DRUG-FREE THERAPEUTIC COMMUNITY

DRUG-FREE THERAPEUTIC COMMUNITY

An Evaluation

Robert C. Brook, Ed.D.
Addiction Research Foundation, London, Canada

Paul C. Whitehead, Ph.D.
University of Western Ontario, London, Canada

HUMAN SCIENCES PRESS
72 Fifth Avenue
NEW YORK, NY 10011
3 Henrietta Street
LONDON, WC2E 8LU

72 Fifth Avenue, New York, New York 10011

Printed in the United States of America
0 987654321

Library of Congress Cataloging in Publication Data

Brook, Robert C
Drug-free therapeutic community.

Bibliography: p.
Includes index.
1. Therapeutic community. 2. Narcotic addicts—Rehabilitation. 3. Amphetamine abuse—Treatment—Ontario—London. 4. Addiction Research Foundation of Ontario. I. Whitehead, Paul C., joint author.
II. Title.
RC489.T67BB76 362.2'9 LC79-20477
ISBN 0-87705-383-9

Life itself still remains
a very effective therapist.

—Karen Horney

Dedicated to

Dr. H. David Archibald

Dr. Charles H. Aharan

CONTENTS

LIST OF FIGURES

LIST OF TABLES

PREFACE

The purpose of this book is threefold. First, we assess the current state of knowledge on the therapeutic community in the treatment of addictions. Second, we describe *414,* a therapeutic community. Third, we present the results of an evaluation of the efficacy of *414* based primarily, but not exclusively, on follow-up assessment of its residents. The follow-ups were conducted 10 months, and again 4 years after treatment.

414, which became known by its address number, was a therapeutic community for young, white working- and middle-class amphetamine abusers. This contrasts the more typical therapeutic community for heroin addicts where residents tend to be older and minority group members. However, its philosophy, structure, and content was typical of that found in other therapeutic communities.

This book only partially captures a larger experience. The same is unfortunately true of our ability to properly acknowledge the many and varied contributions to this endeavor.

The dedication reflects our indebtedness to Dr. H. David

Archibald and Dr. Charles H. Aharan. Dr. Archibald served the Addiction Research Foundation as its Executive Director for over 20 years. Under his guidance and leadership an extremely small, but never inconsequential, operation grew into a provincewide array of facilities and services that has become internationally renowned.

Dr. Charles H. Aharan established the first regional office of the Addiction Research Foundation and served as its Regional Director for almost 20 years. He convinced Dr. Archibald to establish a therapeutic community for amphetamine abusers in London. We have learned much from these men and this dedication is symbolic of our gratitude.

The staff of *414* gave their time, energy, and themselves to a community to help troubled adolescents come to terms with themselves and their environment and develop effective styles of coping to replace their self-destructive patterns of behavior. John Lewis, Jack Kaplun, Paul Sannella, Wayne Thompson, Kathy Evans, Mike Bossin, and Rob Groeneboer earned our thanks and appreciation; but, more importantly, they earned the same from the residents.

Rob Groeneboer and Duncan Cameron served as follow-up workers. It is because of their perseverance and ingenuity that such a sizable protion of our sample was successfully reached, reinterviewed, and retested.

Two Senior Research Assistants invested considerable efforts in various phases of this project. Barbara Szandorowska contributed, over a span of 4 years, to planning the follow-up, analyzing results, and preparing summaries. B. Gail Frankel worked extensively on analysis, writing, and editing early drafts of this manuscript. We are most grateful for their patience and diligence.

Sue and Doreen, our respective spouses, know well the heavy costs that such a project extracts from the psyches and lives of those involved. We thank them for their patience, inspiration, and understanding through the trials associated with this endeavor.

Another family that must be acknowledged is the "family of *414,*" comprised of residents and staff who labored, anguished, and interacted with one another in the hope of growing and helping others to grow, caring, and helping others to care. One of us (R.C.B), as Director of *414,* lived this experience, the other of us has experienced it vicariously. We have both come to appreciate it.

R.C.B.
P.C.W.

Chapter 1

THE THERAPEUTIC COMMUNITY IN HISTORICAL PERSPECTIVE

The use of therapeutic communities in the treatment of drug abuse began with the establishment of Synanon in California in 1958 (Yablonsky, 1965; Deissler, 1970). Many facilities with similar features have since developed in the United States and Canada, as well as in Great Britain and other countries.

In North America, the growth has been extensive. A directory published by the North American Association of Therapeutic Communities (Sack, 1975) listing over 300 such treatment facilities does not constitute an exhaustive catalogue. The growth of the movement has been accompanied by an expanding volume of literature on this topic. This chapter reviews some of that literature, examine's the roots of therapeutic communities and self-help groups, and presents an overview of some of the major therapeutic communities operating in the United States and Canada in terms of their goals, programs, clients, staffing, research, and evaluation.

THE CONCEPT OF "COMMUNITY"

In discussions of therapeutic communities, *therapeutic* has been emphasized to the neglect of the concept of *community.* "Therapeutic" focuses on the objective, that is, being healed, whereas "community" is the means and process used to achieve the objective. The philosophic and social roots of contemporary therapeutic communities reach far back through the centuries. "Community" movements are generally characterized by individuals who group together to realize their individual and collective potential seeking new associations, new opportunities, and a new life. This mobilization frequently springs from some form of discontent, occasionally from persecutions. While these communities are usually formed in reaction to the prevailing social norms, they sometimes reflect the altruistic values of the dominant culture. For example, the Essenes of the first century before Christ were devout Hebrews who separated themselves from apostate Israel to live a communal existence in strict accord to the *Torah.* Benedict organized Western monasticism in the fifth century to live out the *Opus Dei.* In the thirteenth century, Francis became a mendicant to be free from the allures of wealth and the distractions of commerce. In the eighteenth century, Wesley established "cells" for the spiritual growth of the pious. The numerous "communes" throughout the countryside of nineteenth-century France inspired Marx to name his political philosophy communism. Mowrer (1976) points out that Mahatma Gandhi lived and urged others to live in a small intimate type of group or community known as an ashram.

Contemporary therapeutic communities and community movements of the past share many of the following common elements, whether their goals are stated in psychological, religious, or political terms (cf. Glaser, 1977).

1. *Charismatic leadership.* A single visionary who, by sheer force of personality and energy, serves as the focus of

ideals for the group and motivates a style of life consistent with those ideas. The leader is frequently perceived as deviant by the larger society and sometimes as a threat to it. Other positions of authority are usually achieved rather than ascribed.

2. *Order and discipline.* A belief that following the established "rule" promotes individual security and fosters personal and community growth. Members are expected to commit themselves to the routine as a means of becoming free from their capriciousness.

3. *Personal responsibility.* A belief that each person must "own" his or her attitudes and feelings and the consequences of his or her behavior. The capacity for change, growth, or healing reside within the individual; the community provides the environment for its actualization.

4. *Convivial labor.* A belief that survival of the community is based on mutual interdependence. Each member has an integral role to play within the community. All labor, even the most menial is seen as valuable and a direct expression of the individual's creative contribution to the community.

5. *Strict admission standards.* Elaborate entrance procedures may prevail, but even where entrance is easily accomplished, full acceptance into the community is achieved only after extended periods of sustained positive behavior. Status levels are carefully delineated and are accompanied by "rites of passage." Responsibilities and privileges are closely associated.

6. *Public confession.* A belief that a person is liberated from guilt and open to growth by the processes of self-examination, the recognition of fault, "owning" the experience of disappointment, public admission, a resolve to amend delinquency, and a striving for ideals.

7. *Punishment.* A belief that appropriate punishment corrects the individual and provides retribution to the community. Violations of the community's norms are dealt with quickly and forcefully.

8. *Commitment to a life within the community.* A belief that the community provides hope, whereas those who separate

from the community are without hope. Membership in the community means that people are members of a family where they are each other's keeper.

9. *Population size.* An optimum size is associated with the ability of members to know one another or, in some cases, the ability of the community to be economically self-sufficient. While recognized, this is seldom specified. When the size exceeds its natural limits, splinter groups emerge.

10. *Elitism.* The separation of communities from society stems from a sense of being elite, as well as a fear of external contamination. Revisionists are feared and change is slow.

Social Psychiatry and the Therapeutic Community

Maxwell Jones and Therapeutic Community

Salasnek and Amini (1971) trace the idea of the *therapeutic community* back to the *Republic* of Plato, but the term was first used by Thomas Main in 1945 to describe an innovative method of organizing psychiatric hospitals. Main (1946) presents Northfield Hospital in England as a community where staff and patients alike participated fully in the management of the unit with the goal of resocializing patients into the larger society. He examines the implications of social restructuring for traditional roles of physicians and patients in the psychiatric hospital. These roles were more fully articulated later by Maxwell Jones, an English psychiatrist with whom the concept of therapeutic community, in modern social psychiatry, is generally associated (cf. Burke, 1968).

In 1940, Jones was in charge of a 100-bed unit for the study and treatment of neurocirculatory asthenia (effort syndrome) occurring among members of the British Armed Services. Results of studies establishing links between physiological symptoms and emotional conflict were shared with the patients and staff during frequent meetings. The patients began to change their attitudes toward their symptoms as a result of discussions among themselves. New arrivals quickly adopted these attitudes accepting treatment directed to the cause of the conflict, not the symptoms themselves (M. Jones, 1957). This fostered the realization that benefits could be derived from sharing knowledge about causes and treatment of emotional conflict with the patients themselves.

Jones carried this concept to the Social Rehabilitation Unit at Belmont Hospital. Nonpsychiatric patients with personality problems and normal intelligence were presented with a highly structured environment. Large community meetings, therapy groups, and workshops held on a regular basis promoted the exchange of information, the expression of feelings, and the frank and open discussion of both individual and group problems. Privileged communication between patient and physician was discouraged and patients became increasingly involved in their own and in each other's rehabilitation (M. Jones, 1957).

Rapaport (1960) discusses four major themes that characterized the Social Rehabilitation Unit at Belmont Hospital: (1) *democratization*—members have one vote, regardless of status; (2) *permissiveness*—members are expected to tolerate and deal with disturbed behavior, not simply punish it; (3) *communalization*—the sharing of thoughts among members is considered valuable and necessary; and (4) *confrontation*—members are expected to face their problems and deal with the interpretations provided by other members of the group (cf. Clark, 1965).

Salasnek and Amini (1971) underline four additional points in Jones' concept of therapeutic community: (1) the orientation of the group to productive work and a quick return to society, (2) the use of educational techniques and group pressure for constructive purposes, (3) the diffusion of authority from staff to patients, the whole community identifying with the aims, successes, and failures of the unit, and (4) the establishment of open, two-way communication among all members, staff, and patients.

The essential ingredients in Jones' model include the following: open and free communication, the need to share feelings and experiences, an orientation toward productive work, the transfer of some authority from staff to patients, the presence of a charismatic leader, and a core group of long-term patients who bear the major responsibility for the socialization of new members into the community (M. Jones, 1968a; 1976; cf. 1968b; Karasu, Plutchik, Conte, Siegel, & Hertzman, 1977).

George Fairweather and Community Living

After successfully demonstrating problem solving and decision making by mental patients *in* hospitals, George Fairweather and his colleagues attempted to assess the viability of an experiment in community living for mental patients *outside* a hospital setting (Fairweather, Sanders, Maynard, & Cressler, 1969). They established a lodge community of chronic mental patients, providing them with a supportive living situation. The social structure within this community allowed opportunities for meaningful work, status mobility, and a system of rewards and sanctions for the performance of assigned tasks.

Professional staff were in charge of the research project and acted as program consultants. Initially, there was considerable reliance by patients on a staff coordinator, despite the fact that they had demonstrated abilities to make decisions prior to the move from the hospital. As the patients became more cohesive and attained higher status positions, this reliance diminished in accord with the design of the program.

The daily functioning of the lodge was managed by an executive committee of patients. They established two industrial programs: a janitorial and a gardening service, which initially suffered from lack of expertise and poor work attitudes. However, as charismatic figures joined the lodge, many of these problems were overcome and the janitorial service became a successful business.

After 3 years of operation, the lodge program was discontinued and assessed. Results indicated that many of the specific goals of the program had been attained. The lodge members, when compared to a control group, spent significantly more time in the outside community during the period of the lodge's operation and after it closed. They had higher rates of employment during the program, but no differences were found on this measure after the lodge closed. Measures of self-esteem however, did not differentiate the lodge members from the control group, either during the time the lodge was open or after it closed. The experiment demonstrated that psychiatric patients could live together and function well in terms of decision making and employment in this newly created protected environment.

Alcoholics Anonymous and Self-help

Alcoholics Anonymous began in Akron, Ohio, in 1935, with the recovery of two alcoholics, Bill W. and Dr. Bob S. (Alcoholics Anonymous, 1939, 1973). Its organizational principles and beliefs stem from the Oxford Group Movement (cf. Glaser, 1974a) and it developed its own set of traditions that have been retained throughout its 40-year history. A revised history of Alcoholics Anonymous reports the existence of 20,000 A. A. groups in the world with an estimated 650,000 members in 1973 (Alcoholics Anonymous, 1973). While this represents an impressive number of individuals who attribute their sobriety to A. A., the number (or proportion) of persons for whom the A. A. method has not been successful is not known because A. A. has always resisted being evaluated in a scientific manner.

Alcoholics Anonymous operates on the principles outlined as the "Twelve Steps," some of which are self-examination, the admission of personal powerlessness over alcohol, belief and reliance on a power greater than the self, restitution of wrongs done, and carrying the message to others (Alcoholics Anonymous, 1952).

The only involvement of professionals in A. A. is as anonymous members or as volunteers contributing their time and energy to the movement. The "Big Book" (Alcoholics Anonymous, 1939) emphasizes that the key to success resides in the support of peers and that alcoholics are the best people to help other alcoholics. Once members of A. A. achieve sobriety and get their lives in order, their most important role is "Twelfth Step Work," that is, carrying the message of A. A. to others.

Summary

The therapeutic community in the treatment of drug abusers has roots in three separate traditions: the structure and the nature of community described by Jones, Fairweather's notion of a permanent environment outside of institutional settings managed and supported by peers, and the A. A. philosophy of self-help. Together these traditions evolved into a new modality for the treatment of drug abuse, the therapeutic community. While few existing therapeutic communities recognize the contributions of Jones and Fairweather to their development, some do acknowledge A. A. as part of their history, inasmuch as the founder of Synanon, Chuck Dederich, an A. A. member, incorporated much of A. A.'s philosophy into the first community. Most therapeutic communities date their history from 1958 and the establishment of the Synanon Foundation. However, as we have seen, they have a richer history and stem from more complex traditions than is generally recognized.

Major Therapeutic Communities in the Treatment of Drug Abuse: Description

Early treatment programs for drug abuse designed primarily to detoxify heroin addicts (cf. Glasscote, Sussex, Jaffe, Ball, & Brill, 1972) met with little success (Weppner, 1971; 1973; Jones, 1972). Addicts detoxified and discharged to the community soon returned to drug use, often developing larger habits than they had before (cf. Duvall, Locke, & Brill, 1963; Vaillant, 1966). The therapeutic community sought to develop the internal resources of addicts to deal with problems in living, in addition to detoxifying them.[1]

The first and best known of the therapeutic communities is *Synanon,* established by Charles (Chuck) Dederich in Santa Monica, California in 1958 (Yablonsky, 1962; 1965; 1971; Enright, 1970; 1971; Casriel, 1963, Endore, 1968). Dederich, an ex-alcoholic and a member of A.A., began Synanon with a small group of alcoholics who met regularly in his home. As the group grew to include drug addicts, a split occurred between the alcoholics and the addicts, and the addicts began an experiment in community living under Dederich's leadership that led to the establishment of the Synanon Foundation.

Most of the later therapeutic communities owe and credit their beginnings to Synanon, either because they use it as a model or more directly because their programs have been established by ex-members of Synanon, graduates, or persons trained by Synanon. For instance, *Daytop Village* was established in 1963 as an experimental program for addicted felons on parole and it became a workable therapeutic community as a result of the efforts of David Deitch, a Synanon graduate (Devlin, 1975). His arrival and his activities as Director had a major impact on the program. Daytop quickly changed its source of residents and by 1965, opened its doors to voluntary admissions of both sexes.

In 1966, the city of Philadelphia began negotiations with Daytop to open a facility near that city. About this time a major power conflict between David Deitch and Daniel Casriel, the Medical Superintendent, caused some 35 staff members and 200 ex-addicts to leave the community (Casriel & Amen, 1971). One of those who left Daytop, John Ruocco, established *Gaudenzia House* in Philadelphia in 1968 (Glaser, 1971).

Phoenix House was established in 1967 in New York City. A Puerto Rican psychiatrist, Efren Ramirez, successful with a treatment program for addicts in Puerto Rico, was invited by

Mayor John Lindsay to head the Addiction Services Agency in 1967. He started the first Phoenix program, which has since grown into several houses. The Phoenix program shows the influences of a variety of sources: an existential treatment program in Puerto Rico, the Daytop graduate who brought form and strength to the program, a group of Synanon graduates, and the psychoanalytic orientation of Mitchell Rosenthal who became the program's first superintendent (Rosenthal, 1973).

The last of the major therapeutic communities, *Odyssey House,* established in New York in 1966, has more independent origins, but subscribes to most of the basic tenets of the Synanon model. What began as a pilot research program designed to evaluate the use of a narcotic maintenance drug called cyclazocine, in Metropolitan Hospital in New York, developed into a therapeutic milieu that viewed the use of all drugs as antitherapeutic (Densen-Gerber, 1971; 1974). Seventeen ex-addicts and a lawyer-psychiatrist, Judianne Densen-Gerber, moved out of the hospital and established Odyssey House (Murphy and Densen-Gerber, 1971). Odyssey House has treatment goals and staffing patterns that differ somewhat from those in other facilities. It also has a variety of specific programs established to meet special needs of pregnant addicts and addicted parents (Odyssey House Information Centre, a;b;c).

Goals and Objectives of the Program

It is not explicitly stated, but all programs seem to adhere to the general objective articulated for Phoenix House: the changing of inappropriate responses and behavior patterns to more effective and appropriate ones (Rosenthal, 1973). The drug addict's behaivor, viewed as "stupid" by Shelley and Bassin (1965), needs to be modified. Personally responsible for his or her own behavior (cf. Deissler, 1970; Murphy and Densen-Gerber, 1971) the addict is considered capable of change. The attainment of drug-free status, the development of alternative, more effective, life-styles enabling members to cope with problems in living (Collier, Hijazi, Dance, Broudy, Winckler, & Forget, 1973) and reentry, or return to society, are the major objectives shared by most communities (Rosenthal, 1973; Murphy & Densen-Gerber, 1971; Glaser, 1971; System Sciences, Inc., 1973a). A major exception is Synanon, which does not share the objective of reentry. The Synanon Foundation views society as so corrupt that it is not worth reentering (System Sciences, Inc., 1973a). According to Yablonsky (1971), members are adequately prepared to reenter, but many choose not to do so. Synanon has built its own structurally separate society that includes schools for children, work for adults, and facilities of all kinds for all ages to provide a milieu within which residents and graduates of Synanon can pursue an alternative way of living (Yablonsky & Dederich, 1965).

For many, return to society implies a return to a former life-style and social situation. Outside Synanon, drug addicts, regardless of age, sex, or race, tend to occupy low status positions, rarely have legitimate sources of income, and are vulnerable to unemployment and general economic fluctuations. Impoverished educational backgrounds further limit their chances to better their positions. Within Synanon, addicts have positions that afford them a measure of self-respect and the opportunity to earn the respect of others. These factors help to account for the many who choose to remain in Synanon and make it a way of life.[2]

Activites of the Programs

In order to meet their objectives, therapeutic communities developed programs that are different from those of other modalities of treatment.

Synanon is a *peer-oriented* and *peer-controlled* community. Originally established for heroin addicts, it now accepts "squares," nonaddicts who wish to learn to deal with their emotional problems. Professionals are only associated with

Synanon as outside consultants, whose roles are well-defined and generally quite limited (cf. Cherkas, 1965).

Four other therapeutic communities—Daytop, Phoenix, Gaudenzia, and Odyssey—are essentially peer oriented but not totally peer controlled in that professionals are involved along with ex-addict staff in the day-to-day management.

Therapeutic communities utilize meaningful work as a means of providing regular routines for the residents, replacing the drug-taking and drug-seeking cycle with a well-defined regimen of daily tasks. A typical day at Synanon illustrates the routine incorporated by most communities. Variations that occur within some communities reflect differences in objectives.

The Synanon day begins at 6:30 A.M. Members make their beds, wash, and breakfast together (Holzinger, 1965). Near the end of the morning meal a senior member reads a passage from Emerson, Thoreau, or another philosopher. After breakfast members perform assigned tasks ranging from cleaning the house to carrying out senior administrative functions. New members are assigned menial jobs, commensurate with their status. Each resident has a job to do and is expected to perform it well.

After lunch another philosopher is read and discussed by some members, while others gather to practice impromptu public speaking. These brief sessions are considered important for members to learn to discuss ideas, rather than their life on the street. This also trains them for future speaking engagements in the community, a Synanon activity. Members learn to interact with one another on an intellectual level as well as to accept and give constructive criticism (Holzinger, 1965). The content of these discussions is peculiar to Synanon, though the nature of the interaction is not. None of the other therapeutic communities provide such a highly structured forum for discussion and intellectual sharing. After the postlunch meetings, members return to their assigned tasks. The average number of hours per day spent on work by residents of the various therapeutic communities closely approximates the working day in society: Daytop Village, 6.4 hours per day; Phoenix House, 7.8 hours per day; Odyssey House, 7.8 hours per day (System Sciences, Incorporated, 1973a,b,c).

The major therapeutic tool of Synanon and the other therapeutic communities is the *game,* (described in more detail, Chapter 2). Games take the form of encounter therapy sessions where each member, regardless of status, is open to personal criticism and support from fellow residents (cf. Yablonsky, 1965; Yablonsky & Dederich, 1965). There is a no-holds-barred attitude in these sessions; nothing is forbidden except physical violence. The honesty and openness that characterize confrontations in the therapeutic community has been criticized as a form of tyranny (Malcolm, 1973b), but proponents agree that encounter therapy is an essential feature of the therapeutic process.

The amount of time spent in activities defined as counseling or therapy is quite variable. At Synanon, games are held three times a week and they devote 1.5 hours specifically to therapy; Phoenix House spends 3.2 hours per day in therapy; Odyssey House devotes 3.0 hours to therapy daily (System Sciences, Incorporated, 1973a, c). Communities with professional staff spend more time per day in therapeutic activities.

Advocates of the therapeutic community consider a regimented structure to be necessary for maintaining a drug-free existence and to promote a constructive use of time. Some addicts who leave the protective environment of the therapeutic community may experience difficulties in adjusting to a less structured existence in the larger society.

One type of activity designed to reduce the problem of transition is working outside of the therapeutic community while still living in it. Synanon no longer encourages this although it was initially an integral part of the program (Yablonsky, 1965; Endore, 1968). Other communities claim that this is an important part of their program, but available evidence indicates that very little time per day is actually spent working outside: Phoenix House, an average of 3 minutes; Daytop, 20 minutes; and Odyssey, which makes the most consistent claim for adequate reentry preparation, 5 minutes (Systems Sciences, Incorporated, 1973, a,b,c).

Work within therapeutic communities serves as the central mechanism in the establishment and maintenance of a status hierarchy. Theoretically this allows any member starting at the bottom of the work hierarchy doing menial tasks to rise to an executive postion. Witnessing daily changes in the status of other members helps new members to survive the first few weeks (Yablonsky, 1965; Casriel, 1963), and fosters awareness of the necessity to do assigned jobs well. Demotions for infractions of rules, while criticized in the reports of System Sciences, Incorporated for being too arbitrary, commonly occur along with promotions and are seen by some as beneficial (cf. Yablonsky, 1965; Cherkas, 1965; Deissler, 1970).

In addition to demotions, the *haircut,* a form of punishment, is meted out in an actual physical haircut or, more typically, a verbal dressing down in front of the whole community (see, for example, Rosenthal, 1973; Deissler, 1970). Other forms of punishment include ridicule (Casriel & Amen, 1971) and negative sanctions for behavior that is perceived as threatening to the community (Lesser, 1974). The effect of this kind of punishment is somewhat unclear, but reports of Casriel (1963), Yablonsky (1965), and Endore (1968) indicate that residents appear to develop a sense of community and personal responsibility from it.

Procedures for Admission

At Synanon there are some screening procedures for prospective residents, but essentially all addicts who wish to enter are allowed to do so. Fees are charged to some to test their motivation (Endore, 1968) and all are expected to withdraw from drugs without the aid of medication. Withdrawal in the supportive setting is reported to be less painful than addicts expect based on previous experiences on the street, in jails, or in hospitals (Yablonsky, 1965; Casriel & Amen, 1971; cf. Whitehead, 1978). Once they have withdrawn from drugs, usually 24 to 48 hours after admission, residents are expected to assume responsibilities in day-to-day tasks and attend Synanon games. The incidence of people leaving the program prematurely (known as the split rate) is reported to be high during the first few months (Yablonsky, 1962; Casriel, 1963). The common ideology is that the splitters will not be readmitted, but the evidence indicates that those who return and show reasonable levels of motivation are readmitted (Yablonsky, 1965; Endore, 1968).

Admitting procedures at Daytop were originally designed to test the level of the addict's motivation. For instance, an addict referred from the courts was given carfare to the end of the ferry and told to call for the Village bus. Once delivered to the house, the addict was asked to wait on a veranda outside an unlocked door for an hour or more. During this time the addict witnessed former friends (who failed to recognize him or her) in continual activity. When finally called into the office, the addict was confronted by ex-addicts who refused to be conned by him or her (Bassin, 1974). Those who did not leave before or during the interview were usually accepted into the program.

In contrast to the original procedures, the atmosphere is now less threatening and confronting (cf. Collier et al., 1973). As of 1973, admissions to Daytop are handled during a 2-day period through the Screening, Induction, and Referral Unit. At this time, medical examinations are given and psychological, demographic, and drug history data are collected.

Historically, admission procedures involve testing motivation in a confrontative setting involving ex-addict staff. However, this has been in a situation where admissions have been voluntary. A marked change has occurred during the last half of the 1970s. According to Dupont, then Director of the National Institute on Drug Abuse, therapeutic communities have increasingly found themselves with the vast majority of their clients being put there involuntarily through court orders (Tripartite Conference, 1978). No assessments have been made of the implications of this shift, but an earlier study by De Leon et al. (1972) suggested that the rate of improvement was greater on the part of involuntary admissions than for those who admitted themselves voluntarily.

Characteristics of Residents

Information on the characteristics of residents of therapeutic communities is limited. Reportedly all communities have a racial mix and male and female addicts ranging in age from early adolescence to late middle age. The only descriptive data on Synanon date back to 1963 when the resident population is described as 75% white, 16% black, and 9% other; 83% male and 27% female; 2% under age 20, 20% aged between 20 and 24, and 78% 25 and over (Yablonsky & Dederich, 1965).

Available demographic descriptions of the resident populations of Daytop, Phoenix, and Odyssey indicate that all three have more males than females, and fewer whites than members of other racial groups. Odyssey generally has a younger population, as they alone provide special programs for adolescents (see Table 1).

Staffing

A major problem considered to contribute to racial tension, especially at Daytop, is the racial imbalance between residents and staff. Some 80% of the Daytop staff is white compared to only 43% of the residents (System Sciences, Incorportated, 1973a).

At both Phoenix and Daytop, the proportions of female clients and staff are similar, but these communities have been criticized for not providing appropriate role models for females and it is said that women residents were not adequately pre-

Table 1.1 Distribution of Residents by Race, Sex and Age for Phoenix House, Daytop Village and Odyssey House, 1973

	Phoenix House[a]		*Daytop Village*[b]		*Odyssey House*[c]	
	No.	*Percent*	*No.*	*Percent*	*No.*	*Percent*
Race						
White	78	26	161	43	54	41
Black	179	61	177	47	70	43
Hispanic	35	12	38	10	8	6
Other	2	1	1	1	—	—
Sex						
Male	225	76	375	84	83	63
Female	69	24	70	16	49	37
Age						
15 and under	4	1	6	2	30	23
16 to 20	100	34	164	37	38	29
21 and 25	115	39	184	41	43	33
25 and over	75	26	91	20	21	16

[a]Demographic characteristics of residents who were interviewed (System Sciences, Incorporated, 1973b).
[b]Census of Residents, January 1973 (System Sciences, Incorporated, 1973a).
[c]Description of Residents, April 1973 (System Sciences, Incorporated, 1973c).

pared to assume other than the traditional female roles (System Sciences, Incorporated, 1973a; 1973b). It has been recommended that women be made aware of nontraditional types of employment and educational opportunities available to them on reentry.

The staffing problems reported at Odyssey House are of a different nature. Odyssey has a large proportion of professional staff who, according to policy, are not involved in the peer-controlled disciplinary structure, but who devote full time to therapy. Contrary to policy, however, many professionals do get involved (System Sciences, Incorporated, 1973c). This results in conflict and confusion for the nonprofessional ex-addict staff members, whose roles become less clearly delineated, as well as for the residents who depend on the disciplinary structure of the community.

There is an intensifying rivalry between professional staff and ex-addict staff within the therapeutic community movement. The fundamental issue is who will control the therapeutic communities? Ex-addict staff tend to believe that the experiences they have acquired, first as addicts and then as residents who have lived drug-free, are sufficient credentials for being members of staff in therapeutic communities. The involvement of professionals has shifted the emphasis from the importance of personal experiences to an emphasis on professional and academic credentials (De Leon & Breschner, 1976). This rivalry was evident at the World Congress of Therapeutic Communities held in Montreal in 1977 and it constitutes a potential schism within the movement.

Sources of Financial Support

Synanon exists entirely on donations from friends and proceeds from solicitation of funds by members (Yablonsky, 1965; Endore, 1968; Mueller, 1964). Admission fees as much as $1000 are charged to addicts and to "squares" seeking entry into Synanon (Endore, 1968; Glaser, 1971). The Synanon Foundation does not draw on public funds in order to avoid government control of the program (Endore, 1968). Synanon prides itself on financial independence, living the ideal of individual responsibility. Initially Synanon's financial structure was precarious (Yablonsky, 1965), but this no longer appears to be the case (Endore, 1968).

Available data on the sources of Gaudenzia's financial support indicate that the City of Philadelphia, the state of Pennsylvania, and other public agencies contribute to the organization (Glaser, 1971). The exact contributions are unknown to us.

Daytop, Phoenix, and Odyssey receive both public and private funding from a variety of sources. This includes the City of New York and various federal sources such as the Office of Economic Opportunity and the National Institute of Mental Health (Systems Sciences, Incorporated, 1973a; 1973b; 1973c). These three programs are considered to provide a considerable savings to New York, compared to the economic costs of maintaining addicts in prisons, or the average cost to society of the addict's drug habits (System Sciences, Incorporated, 1973a; 1973b; 1973c). For example, the per diem rate at Phoenix House is $10 or half the cost of jail in New York City (System Sciences, Incorporated, 1973b).

At Daytop, the cost per person day of treatment is about $21 (System Sciences, Incorporated, 1973a). The drug habits of Odyssey House clients before treatment cost $48 per day, treatment averages about $19 per day, representing an apparent savings of almost $30 per day per person (System Sciences, Incorporated, 1973c). Such savings should be interpreted cautiously as they usually fail to take into account periods of enforced or voluntary abstinence. A drug habit is not always supported through such illegal means as stealing, but frequently involves the selling of drugs to other addicts.

Discussion

The specific objectives of the therapeutic community are to achieve drug-free status for all its members, to change individual life-styles, and to either prepare the residents for reentry into the larger society or provide them with a structurally separate alternative society. Adequate preparation for reentry, however, appears to be a problem. It is unclear whether residents acquire sufficient social and economic skills to survive the transition from the therapeutic community to the larger society. Few follow-up studies have adequately assessed the success of reentry.

Major Therapeutic Communities in the Treatment of Drug Abuse: Evaluation

Are therapeutic communities successful in attaining their objectives and achieving their goals?

Synanon considers empirical research an inappropriate means of assessing a program's efficacy. According to Yablonsky and Dederich (1965) Synanon must be understood in terms of its own conceptual framework and not forced into traditional research constructs. Members are too busy and "unable to answer questions" for researchers (Mueller, 1964). Accordingly, while an early study reports that 72% of the first 263 admissions to Synanon left before completing the 2-year program, and that clients who stayed remained drug free in proportion to the time spent in the program (Volkman & Cressey, 1963), they do not indicate the length of the follow-up period if one was used, or whether residents returned to society.

Various studies describe the history of Gaudenzia (Glaser, 1971; 1974a) and evaluate different aspects of its program (Lesser, 1974; McKee, Lehigh, & Miller, 1971). Lesser (1974) observed that as time in the program increased, the number of episodes of physical illness decreased, and the type of illness considered serious by the resident changed. These findings imply that members no longer use illness as a means of avoiding responsibility, but the lasting effect of this aspect of resocialization can not be assessed without follow-up data.

McKee et al. (1971) report that younger, unmarried addicts who speak and understand English have a better chance of completing the Gaudenzia program than Teen Challenge and a methadone maintenance program to which it was compared. Based on these results, they contend that more care in admission procedures and fitting addicts to programs would insure better treatment results for therapeutic communities in terms of completing the program. Follow-up on other outcome criteria, such as duration of changes in dealing with problems of living and maintaining a drug-free status and employment are not mentioned.

According to Glaser (1974b) one of the critical measures of the success of a therapeutic community is its holding power or its ability to retain residents long enough to have an effect on them. The reciprocal of this is the *split rate,* or the proportion of new admissions who leave a program against the advice of staff in a given period of time. Glaser examined the problem of attrition at Gaudenzia for the 5 years of its existence. Annual rates calculated on the first 2 years, and monthly rates from January 1971 indicate that splitting is "frequent, early, and variable." About 80 of evey 100 admissions to Gaudenzia leave and do not return. Half terminate by the end of the first month, two-thirds by the second month, three-quarters by the third, and four-fifths by the end of the fourth month.

Glaser suggests that high rates of attrition are unacceptable to practitioners. He offers countermeasures to increase the likelihood of a resident staying long enough to develop ties to a program. He suggests stringent selection procedures, and using methadone as an adjunct to the treatment program during the early months. Gaudenzia has implemented selective admission policies that are calculated to reduce the split rate. They admit only those addicts who are legally compelled to complete their sentence at Gaudenzia.

In a study of the Daytop program, Collier (1973a) differentiates between addicts who leave the program prematurely and those who complete it. Completers are more likely to be white, middle class, with a higher education, previous military service, for whom the drug choice is heroin. Those whose drug of choice is a nonnarcotic (amphetamines or barbiturates) are the least likely to complete the program. No conclusions are drawn concerning the implications of these findings for the program as a whole. No measure of outcome other than completion of the program is used.

Results of a second study indicate that those with prior

treatment in methadone programs are more likely to either stay longer or complete the program than those who either experienced other kinds of treatment or no treatment prior to Daytop. Collier (1973b) concludes that these results support the inclusion of methadone maintenance as a component of treatment in therapeutic communities.

Collier and Hijazi (1973), in a study of attitudes toward Daytop, found residents expressing a need for better medical care, better job training, more individual counseling, and better preparation for reentry. Residents were dissatisfied with the sexual and racial imbalance between staff and clients and staff attitudes toward residents in the later phases of treatment.

Collier and Hijazi (1974) report the results of the first of a series of longitudinal follow-up studies, designed to last 4 years, on former residents who either completed or dropped out of the Daytop program. Of the former residents asked to participate in the study (272 graduates and 280 dropouts with a minimum 6 months in treatment) a total of 173 graduates and 78 dropouts responded. Long-term graduates ($N = 47$) who had been out of the program for more than 5 years were excluded from the analysis.

Information on the current status of former residents with respect to adjustment in society, post-Daytop involvement with drugs, alcohol and criminal activities, and involvement with work and school was obtained by six interviewers who were matched with clients in terms of age, sex, and ethnicity. External criteria such as information from social and legal agencies and the grapevine of street sources provided reliability checks on the responses.

Age was the only demographic variable found to significantly differentiate respondents from nonrespondents, in that graduate respondents were older, and dropout respondents were younger than nonrespondents.

The respondents report greater problems in readjustment to society, the longer the time in the program (78% of the graduates, 92% of the dropouts). Other problems experienced were reconciling the teachings of the program to the social realities of life and general difficulties in the areas of employment, family, and heterosexual relationships. Most report being employed or in school (92% of graduates, 89% dropouts) and drug free (94% graduates, 53% dropouts) with only infrequent use of alcohol or marijuana. Those who returned to drug use (38 respondents) used a variety of drugs on a regular basis. While criminal involvement has declined, dropouts were more likely to be convicted for selling drugs or theft, and graduates were more likely charged, but not convicted, for minor violations.

The major reasons given for dropouts for leaving the program were favoritism by staff, pressures of the therapeutic process, sexual restrictions, diminished need for therapy, and age differences among residents.

Based on data from this initial follow-up, respondents who were favorably evaluated tended to be older, female, and long-term drug users in both the graduate and dropout categories. Time out of the program made no difference to both groups, but total time in treatment (12 to 18 months) was related to a favorable evaluation for the dropouts only.

According to System Sciences (1973a), a Daytop graduate is one who has demonstrated the ability to "lead a successful productive lifestyle, without recidivism to self-abuse [*sic.*] and/or the abuse of others." As of January 1973 there were 400 graduates, 21 splitters who had left the program before attaining graduate status, but who had met the criteria, and 31 treatment failures (undefined). Fifty percent of the graduates are reportedly employed in fields unrelated to drug addiction, 26% work in related fields, and 10% are employed by Daytop. The biggest problem of adjustment reported by Daytop graduates is the difficulty in securing employment or entering school upon leaving the therapeutic community, a difficulty that *increases* with time spent in the program.

Although only the first phase has been reported, the longitudinal follow-up study at Daytop appears to be a research endeavor of good quality addressing itself to key questions. Relocating respondents for additional follow-ups may not be problematical, given adequate resources and the past success of other researchers (cf. Ball, 1975; Ogborne and Melotte, 1977; Levinson, 1977).

With the high proportion of professional staff members and the diversity of programs offered, Odyssey House would appear to be fruitful ground for research activities. While research is apparently being conducted, the lack of published information is a major criticism of the research program at Odyssey.

According to the 1974 Annual Report (Densen-Gerber, 1974), 98% of those who complete the Odyssey program and 50% of those who stay in treatment for at least 6 months, remain drug free. The report does not adequately describe the methodology involved in the follow-up study and the data are insufficient to evaluate the program's efficacy.

Rohrs, Murphy, & Densen–Gerber (1972) report 2500 admissions to Odyssey House over a 4-year period, with 72% of those remaining beyond the first week completing the program. The dropout rate is 45% during the first week and 28% during treatment. Of these, 50% become readdicted, 20% were found drug free, and 30% were lost to follow-up. During the first 3 years of operation, the program claims 41 drug-free "graduates." The data presented in this report are mystifying. While the length of the program and what constitutes graduation is not known, a report of only 41 graduates in 3 years is ambiguous and inconsistent with the other statistics provided. The report assumes, but does not demonstrate, the effectiveness of Odyssey House and as such is difficult to interpret. Rohrs, Goldsmith, & Densen-Gerber (1971) report on a follow-up study of 120 dropouts at Odyssey House between February and June 1970. Attempts were made to secure data by mail and phone on drug status, employment status, and reasons for leaving the program, which was then reliably checked with information received from key informants. Residents on whom no information was available were considered to be using drugs.

Results showed recidivism to be 100% for those who were in the program for less than 3 months. Among those who stayed more than 3 months, 50% were found to be drug free (Rohrs et al., 1971). Data on employment status and reasons for leaving are not reported.

Although methodologically sound, the study omits information necessary for a critical evaluation of the program's efficacy relative to its goals and objectives. The length of the follow-up period, the comparative proportion of drug-free graduates, and the proportion of all dropouts represented by the sample is information that is required and missing.

Phoenix House has the greatest range of published research material (see, for example De Leon, 1974a; Baise, 1971; De Leon, Rosenthal, & Brodney, 1971; De Leon et al., 1972; De Leon, Skodol, & Rosenthal, 1973; Kaufman & De Leon, 1978). Part of the research focuses on the differences between splitters and those who stay in treatment, from a variety of perspectives including the following: demographic characteristics (De Leon, 1974a); results of psychological testing, specifically the Multiple Affect Adjective Check List (Baise, 1971); ratings of emotionality (De Leon et al., 1971); and criminal activity (De Leon et al., 1973; De Leon, 1974b; Wexler & De Leon, 1977). These studies attempt to identify predictors of who remains in treatment and collect data on admission. The assumption underlying these studies is that remaining in the program is an appropriate measure of efficacy.

Other studies of Phoenix House have followed up splitters and attempted to assess whether time spent in treatment is associated with improvement later on. Two of these are discussed here and a third is mentioned later. In one study, dropouts were interviewed about 5 years after they left Phoenix House and were asked to report retrospectively their status as to drug use, criminal activity, and employment for 6-month intervals that included 12 months and 6 months before they entered Phoenix House and up to 60 months after they left

Phoenix House (De Leon, 1978). The following results were obtained. Addicts reported that they experienced higher rates of drug use and criminal activity and lower rates of employment during the year before treatment than for any time after treatment. There appears to be no significant difference in the level of the reported rates of these behaviors at any of the 6-month intervals after the end of treatment. This may well be a result of the methodology that involves retrospective self-reports over an extended period of time.

The respondents who were followed up were divided into categories based on the amount of time that they had spent in treatment. De Leon (1978) claims that the analysis he presents reveals "a systematic relationship between improvement and time spent in the therapeutic community . . ." on the basis of these retrospective data. We find this claim to be resistible even if one assumes that there are no methodological problems with the data. De Leon's own data indicate the following facts. When functioning among dropouts is measured after they have left the program and is compared to their level of functioning before they entered the program, De Leon found that even persons who spent very little time in the program display marked improvement. Furthermore, there tends to be an absence of significant differences in levels of performance across categories of persons grouped on the basis of the amount of time that they spent in treatment.

A second study focused on psychological test scores of Phoenix residents (De Leon et al., 1973). A cross-sectional analysis indicated that persons in the earliest stages of the program had higher (more pathological) scores than persons who had been in the program longer. Even small differences in time in treatment at times led to marked differences in test scores. However, this cannot be taken as an indication that time in treatment leads to improvements in psychological functioning since fairly marked decreases in pathology occur with exposure to very little treatment. De Leon et al. (1973) also conducted a follow-up study of these residents and their psychopathology scores and their findings are consistent with the interpretation provided above. That is, there was no significant relationship between change in psychopathology scores and time in program:

> Thus, the longitudinal data are impressive in showing that pathology scores consistently and significantly dropped for subjects during the intervening treatment period irrespective of their stage in the Phoenix Program (De Leon et al., 1973).

Vaillant (1974) and Lennard and Allen (1973) question the use of single measures of outcome and the nature of outcome measures generally. They suggest that the goal of treatment, viewed as an ongoing process, should be enduring changes in life-style that can be measured over time. A clear operationalization of success, be it maintenance of drug-free status, the return to family living, or to employment, must be quantifiable and measured at several points in time. The longitudinal follow-up study at Daytop makes some positive advances in this regard. Therapeutic communities must decide what aspects of their program need to be evaluated. If retention is the crucial "outcome," then existing research is in the right direction. It seems, however, that this is insufficient as an exclusive measure of success.

It is evident that research activities are not considered important for most therapeutic communities. Existing research is of limited value in answering the basic question of their effectiveness in altering maladaptive coping mechanisms. Brecher and Consumer Reports (1972) conclude from studies that therapeutic communities are unsuccessful. Smart (1974) reports methodological problems and failure to use control groups in a review of some 20 studies dealing with treatment outcome in therapeutic communities. He indicates that many studies base recovery rates on graduates, not on total admissions, producing inflated rates. Moreover, rates of recovery among graduates vary from 33 to 92% while rates of recovery among splittees vary from 22 to 50%.

The Canadian Scene

According to the Commission of Inquiry into the Non-Medical Use of Drugs, the 28 therapeutic communities operating in Canada as of February 1973 had a maximum residential capacity of 634, with 379 residents in treatment at that time. There were an estmated 15,000 opiate-dependent persons in Canada and many users of other drugs (Le Dain, 1973). Only a small proportion of this population is treated in therapeutic communities, the larger and better known being the X-Kalay Foundation in British Columbia and the Portage Program for drug dependencies in Quebec.

X-Kalay

X-Kalay began in the British Columbia penitentiary system in 1966 as the Indian Education Club. This grew into a halfway house for Indians leaving prison and was eventually established as a therapeutic community for drug abusers. In 1974, X-Kalay had facilities in British Columbia and Manitoba with plans for expansion into Alberta (Berner, 1974).

Financial support for the Foundation comes from a variety of federal and provincial grants and from several businesses owned and operated by Foundation members.

X-Kalay, modeled after Synanon, employs many of its therapeutic techniques including "games," seminars, speaking engagements, and hierarchy of status that is closely tied to work. The cardinal rules of the community are no drugs, no violence, and acceptable performance at assigned tasks. The goals and objectives of the Foundation are not specified, but there is no reason to expect differences from other therapeutic communities.

Prospective members enter X-Kalay on a 30-day trial basis. If judged likely to benefit from the program, they are admitted as undergraduates. Residents are required to master every job within the community and encouraged to further their education outside the community. After six months, graduate status is granted if residents demonstrate good job performance and involvement in other community activities. Only about half of the undergraduates achieve graduate status at this time; the others remain eligible for review at 30-day intervals (Berner, 1974).

Graduates either assume executive positions with the Foundation or work outside and gradually reduce their involvement with the community until they leave officially, about two years after entering. X-Kalay offers an alternative community for members who choose to remain. It includes schools for children and business opportunities for adult members.

No data are available to indicate the size of the community and the characteristics of its residents and staff, or to enable an evaluation of its effectiveness.

Portage

The Portage Program for Drug Dependencies, established in February 1973, grew directly out of the Daytop tradition with a former staff member as its Executive Director and a program similar to Daytop Village. Its therapeutic goals are abstinence from drugs, psychological rehabilitation, improved social functioning and reentry (Devlin, 1975; Devlin and Vamos, 1974). The staff is a mixture of professionals and paraprofessionals (ex-addicts).

The initial report on the first twenty months of operation (Devlin and Vamos, 1974) indicate that of 111 admissions about 13% or 15 persons have completed the program and two-thirds dropped out. These dropouts were slightly older, had a longer history of drug use and were more likely to be French-speaking than those who completed the program.

Plans outlined for follow-up studies of dropouts and those who complete the program indicate an interest in research and evaluation at Portage (Devlin and Vamos, 1974) although they do not appear to have developed operational criteria of success.

Since its inception Portage has been based in Quebec. However, it now plans to expand to Ontario where it will adapt its program to a residential farm where a woodworking shop will be a major activity (Marshall, 1978).

Matsqui

Le Dain (1972) reports a costly evaluation of an experiment conducted at Matsqui, a prison institution for the treatment of drug-dependent persons. This sophisticated, well-controlled study provided a therapeutic community for one group of inmates, and no treatment beyond the usual prison routine for a control group. Results indicate that after release from prison, those exposed to the therapeutic community were *more* likely to be engaged in illegal employment and illegal use of opiates than the inmates who received no special treatment. In fact, the chief investigator of the Matsqui project concluded the program inadvertently promoted a well-adjusted, well-educated dope fiend (Le Dain, 1972).

Conclusions

Therapeutic communities developed as a partial response to the problem of drug abuse in North America, and as an alternative to seemingly inadequate forms of treatment. The goal of these communities is to change ineffective responses and patterns of behavior into more effective ones. Specifically, they seek to help addicts withdraw from the use of drugs, remain drug free, and modify their style of life in such a way that they are better equipped to deal with the problems of everyday living. Synanon has, as one of its objectives, the establishment of an alternate society and the integration of its members into that society, while most of the other therapeutic communities hope to rehabilitate members to make possible their return to the larger society.

Therapeutic communities have very limited appeal to the estimated 300,000 addicts in the United States, according to Brecher et al. (1972), consequently only the most highly motivated are selected as the best bets for cure. Sack (1974) reports that therapeutic communities are an accepted part of the national health system and provide 15% of the treatment for drug dependence in the United States. Cohen (1974), on the other hand, suggests that only 2% of the drug-dependent population is suited for treatment with the therapeutic community model.

Many thousands of persons have had some contact with various therapeutic communities over the past decade or so, however, very little is known about the efficacy of these programs either in absolute terms or in comparision with other therapeutic settings. Nevertheless, according to Sack (1974) and Dupont (1977), therapeutic communities are an accepted part of the national health system.

Chapter 2

BACKGROUND, STRUCTURE, AND CONTENT OF *414*

Canada never had as serious a problem of heroin addiction as did the United States. With the exception of Vancouver, large cities such as Montreal and Toronto had few problems prior to the mid 1960s. Canada, however, was not spared the explosion of drug use manifest in the late 1960s. Many people, especially those under the age of 25, tried for the first time drugs such as marihuana, lysergic acid diethylamide (LSD), amphetamines, barbiturates, and, of course, alcohol. A small proportion, but an alarming number, developed dependencies and experienced social, mental, or physical problems as a result of using these substances.

In order to deal with the emerging drug problem of 1969 and 1970, existing community services were modified, innovative services were created, and new kinds of treaters evolved. Drop-in centers for the management of reactions ranging from drug overdosage to drug-induced hallucinatory experiences were funded by government and operated by young, streetwise people. Since many drug people were disillusioned with traditional health care services, they came to rely on this new breed of young and drugwise helpers as *the experts* in dealing with what was perceived as a new social and medical phenomenon. Malcolm (1975) characterized this era as the golden age of the "magic humanists" who promised instant cures.

During this period, many young people used emergency departments of general hospitals to recuperate from acute psychotic reactions or to manipulate naive physicians into writing prescriptions for them. This new type of patient, who appeared intoxicated, exhibited paranoia, and refused to be touched, placed a strain on hospital workers by being loud, demanding, and unruly. They challenged the hospital system, ignored rules, refused to follow routines, and generally used the hospital as a hotel, shouting down attendants and staff, and upsetting other patients.

These conditions were exacerbated when conflicts emerged among hospital staff. Some physicians and nurses were perceived as aligning themselves with the young rebels. Others, experiencing the situation as out of control, sought transfers, called in the police, discharged young clients as soon as possible, or established order by medicating these young and unruly patients.

One Community's Reaction

London is a fairly prosperous community in southwestern Ontario about 120 miles west of Toronto and east of Detroit. In 1970 its population was just under 200,000. It is an academic community, with the University of Western Ontario being the largest single employer. Insurance companies, trust companies, and light industries contribute a clean community atmosphere. The "forest city," known for its tree-lined streets and parks has little pollution, a competent and fair police force, and offers a generally good quality of life. London is a quiet and conservative community reminiscent of many American middle-size cities of the Eisenhower era. Consequently the drug scene was a wrenching experience that catapulted London into the turbulent 1960s.

As in the case of many other communities, London responded to the drug scene on many fronts. There were demands for more law enforcement and stiffer penalties for users and pushers. Citizen cooperation was encouraged by offering rewards to people who might call in information about drug pushers. Existing treatment services were expanded and some new ones were created in order to meet newly perceived needs. London even tried to integrate and coordinate services for adolescent drug abusers through a network of treatment services.

Experimentation with marihuana, LSD, STP, and other hallucinogens popular at this time resulted in increased needs for assistance by naïve users unable to understand or deal with their altered perceptions, and became a source of public and parental concern. Regular users of high doses of metamphetamine, injected intravenously, were the most troublesome patients to those delivering treatment. Speed freaks, as they became known, tended to be rejected by treatment personnel as "impossible" and by other young people of the drug subculture as "crazy." They were considered "sure failures" for treatment because they were manipulative, appeared psychopathic, and exacerbated the frustration experienced by workers in the field of addictions.

Short-term treatment and outpatient services seemed inappropriate for dealing successfully with chronic, high-dose amphetamine abusers. A therapeutic milieu that was long-term, residential, and structured seemed necessary to deal with the manipulative adolescents. *414* was an attempt to meet these conditions.

The *414* Facility

As with most therapeutic communities, *414* (named for its street address) was located in the downtown area in an older home. It was built at the turn of the century for one of the established families of London. Its construction was elaborate with decorative woodwork, leaded glass windows, crystal chandeliers, and six large fireplaces. A private residence until the late 1950s, it was sold and used as an outpatient clinic for the Middlesex County Mental Health Association, and later resold and modified to serve as a nursing home. The Addiction Research Foundation purchased the building in the spring of 1970. The basement area was modified to produce several offices and a large recreation room. The attic and maid's quarters were remodeled to create additional bedrooms, group rooms, and expanded bathroom facilities. The kitchen area was extensively renovated but maintained a familylike environment.

Despite modifications, the basic style of *414* remained that of a private home with 6000 square feet of elegant carpeted living space spread over four floors. Large bedrooms served well as dormitories for five or six bunk beds. A dining room, large enough to seat the entire *414* community, was graced with a large fireplace, crystal chandeliers, a large bay window, and easy access to a veranda that spanned the front and side of the house. Floor-to-ceiling windows allowed in much natural light, fresh air, and a good view of other homes.

Our next door neighbor was the mayor of London, who always took a special interest in the "family next door." The mayor's support and the fact that *414* was professionally and institutionally an integral part of the community led to our being accepted in the neighborhood. In marked contrast to some other therapeutic communities, *414* never had to fight court battles to move into or stay in the neighborhood.

Peer-Based Structure

All therapeutic communities are *peer oriented* in that residents are expected to be an active part of the process of treatment. They are held responsible for their own success and that of other members. Their role is to share, support, monitor, and confront one another.

In addition to being peer oriented, some therapeutic communities are also *peer controlled,* in that the residents themselves manage the community. They are responsible for budget, expenditure, fundraising, discipline, and all other aspects of administration, eschewing the use of professionals.

In contrast, *414* was organized by a staff of professionals, principally because there were no ex-addicts at that time who were inclined to participate in such a venture. This sizable reliance on professionals makes *414* a peer-oriented, but not a peer-controlled, therapeutic community.

There was considerable respect for the peer-controlled Synanon model in the discussions that were part of organizing *414*, but there was also a strong sense of the sizable role professionals had to play in setting the standards, serving as role models, and organizing the routine of the community in the initial stages of *414*'s development. Consequently, the operational model of *414* was Daytop Village, which includes professionals as integral to the process of treatment, allowing and encouraging a responsible and cooperative relationship among ex-addicts and professional staff.

Four persons constituted the core staff. The director of *414* had extensive experience in the areas of psychology, education, theology, and corrections. His involvement with drug addicts included the organization and operation of a therapeutic community within the Michigan State Department of Corrections and several years with Synanon Houses in Detroit and California. Other staff were professional counselors with the Addiction Research Foundation, an experienced counselor of young people in the local drug scene who was trained in psychology, another experienced as a parole officer within the community, and the third a recent university graduate with some counseling experience. Despite their lack of experience with therapeutic community, these three had good rapport with local youth and a deep commitment to the program.

From September to December 1970, this core staff planned the organization of the therapeutic community, got to know one another through encounter groups, remodeled the facility, and conducted outpatient therapy groups for young people who might later become residents of the house. They also visited other therapeutic communities in New York City.

The first residents were admitted to *414* in December 1970. During the next months, four additional staff were hired to alleviate the pressures of providing 7-days-a-week, 24-hour-a-day supervision as well as meeting other responsibilities. One of these, a young woman familiar with drug abusing adolescents, was hired mostly because she could provide a female role model to the young women with whom she worked.

Unlike most therapeutic communities *414* was amply funded. Internal responsibility for disbursements was shared by staff members and some senior residents.

Indecisiveness on the question of peer control presented certain problems. Interestingly enough, however, they did not involve a struggle for power between the residents and the professional staff. Quite the opposite was true. Periodically, the staff would withdraw from day-to-day direction of the therapeutic community and expect senior residents to move into the breach and take on greater responsibility. Now and then some senior residents would do this, but only for a short time. Even then, the typical pattern was for them to feel imposed on, and to slack off while blaming the staff for not doing its job.

For their part, the staff was disappointed with the lack of energy and initiative shown by the senior residents and would call a meeting to let the residents know that the staff was going to get tough and the slacking off would have to stop. The situation had little to recommend it, and when it occurred, resulted in inconsistent practices.

Levels

Therapeutic communities are organized into levels or statuses that correspond to phases of the program. On the basis of their performance, residents can be promoted to higher levels or demoted to lower ones. Responsibilities, privileges, and expectations vary by status level. There is no fixed period of time spent at each level; instead, moves are made when the resident, peers, and staff agree that the residents are ready. The *414* program is divided into four levels: probationary, junior residency, senior residency, and reentry.

Level I: Probationary Status

Probationary status lasts about 1 to 4 weeks. Detoxification is accomplished nonchemically through the support of peers and by engaging in work. During this time probationers become familiar with the three rigidly enforced rules of the house: no drugs, no violence, and no sexual contact. All tasks necessary to sustain and maintain the treatment community are shared by the members, with neophytes assigned to the most menial chores. While they may later take on more challenging jobs, newcomers are made to understand that they will not be taken care of: they must earn their own way.

The probationary period is a time of high risk for residents. Their investment in the program is low, they still feel like outsiders, and the temptation to return to the street is great. For this reason their behavior is closely scrutinized and much emphasis is placed on integrating them into the life of the community. Many do not make a satisfactory adjustment and at this stage they often split and go back to the street. Those who stay and appear to be adjusting well are promoted to residency status.

Levels II and III: Junior and Senior Residency

Promotion to residency status (junior residents, Level II; senior residents, Level III) is decided by the probationer's peers who have already achieved residency or are at the reentry level in consultation with staff members. Promotion is contingent on convincing these people that the probationer is serious about changing his or her life-style. Total time in residency ranges from 6 to 10 months.

During this period, the residents' behavior, beliefs, and attitudes continue to be evaluated by peers and staff. Residents earn privileges, such as writing letters or receiving visits from family members, by seeking and competently discharging additional responsibilities. They settle into the routine of the community and come to appreciate the rewards and sanctions contingent on various types of behavior. They learn how to accept help from others and how to provide it to others. It is not unusual for residents to be promoted to senior status, demoted to junior status for violation of rules, and repromoted to senior status after another period of responsibile behavior.

Residents complete the senior level of residency when they are coping effectively in the therapeutic community and are prepared to make further adjustments to the world outside.

Level IV: Reentry

The stage of reentry, Level IV, is designed to facilitate transition to the larger community. During this phase, residents continue to live in the therapeutic community and take part in many aspects of its therapeutic and social life, but they attend school or work outside the house. Working or studying in the larger community provides an opportunity to test one's skills in coping with real life. At the same time, since residents remain a part of the therapeutic community where they occupy positions of high status and responsibility, temporary setbacks in the outside world are less likely to be experienced as crushing or ego deflating. The reentry stage lasts about 4 or 5 months and, at its completion, the resident graduates. Graduates either leave the therapeutic community completely or become nonresident staff members.

Peer orientation (with staff involvement) and stratification of residents into levels of treatment are the major structural features of the *414* therapeutic community program. The structure must, of course, be animated by content in order to constitute a program. The main components of this content are the principles on which treatment is based.

CONTENT OF THE *414* PROGRAM

In essence, a therapeutic community is a self-help milieu in which persons experiencing problems in living come together in a residential setting in order to make changes in their own style of coping with life and to help others to do the same. As the name suggests, treatment is the *raison d'etre* that is effected through the social entity of the community. In this respect one is always *in treatment* while in residence. The sense of community is so intense that the group is referred to as a family and interaction among its members is part of the treatment process.

As in the case of other subcultures, therapeutic communities develop a jargon or argot called colloquialisms expressing their basic principles. Special therapy sessions, in the form of encounter groups called games, form another unique aspect of the therapeutic community milieu applied to the treatment of drug abusers. Colloquialisms and games reflect the content of life in *414* and most other therapeutic communities.

COLLOQUIALISMS

The essential principles on which a therapeutic community is based are frequently captured in the day-to-day use of colloquialisms.[1] Such catch phrases, cursory comments, or maxims were operative at *414*, the principal ones being: "no cop-outs," "act as if," "turn around," and "no free lunch." As residents progress through the different levels and become more integrated into the family, they come to have a deeper understanding of these colloquialisms and their underlying principles.

No Cop-outs

A favorite technique for removing the onus of responsibility from oneself is to cop out or blame one's condition on other persons or on unspecified forces. Causes of trouble, hurt, or discomfort are attributed to parents, friends, or the community. Rationalizations are presented as excuses for the problems being experienced. The rationalizations are articulated as "It is not my problem . . . it is someone else's fault and I am stuck with the consequences," and "my situation is beyond my control."

It is true that in many instances antecedent sources of a person's dysfunctional state can be identified (Brook, Szandorowska, & Whitehead, 1976). Many residents had backgrounds of fractured or disorganized families (Whitehead & Brook, 1973), premature sexual experiences often in the form of incest, and psychologically or physically absent parents. Some trace their difficulties to friends who offered acceptance only in conformity to group drug-taking behaviors. Others, who have become disillusioned with school or work, view these endeavors as manifestations of a plastic world that has no meaningful place for them.

Gathering information at intake often conveys to the applicant the misperception that historical events that led to admission *constitute the problem* that is, the current situation is beyond control, or acting-out behavior is understandable in view of the social and emotional disadvantages of the past. In the therapeutic community, such scapegoating behavior is seen as the essence of *copping out.*

Historical events may have etiological significance in the development of the present condition, but they cannot be altered. What can be altered is the attitude about these events. Self-talk is what a person says to himself or herself about past experiences. It keeps past events and experiences alive and part of the present. One's current situation is often in large measure a function of the way in which former events and circumstances are defined, reinforced, and kept alive. Using them as the means of excusing current inaction or self-destructive behavior is countertherapeutic. For example, "I've failed to give up dope in the past" may be an innocent observation with respect to history or it may be a "setup" with the person really saying, "because I've failed in the past,I will fail today or in the future." These and other statements such as "I can't succeed," or "life is trouble," "I don't care," "if only such and such hadn't happened" are the stuff out of which self-fulfilling prophecies are made.

Therapists must resist the temptation to reinforce such rationalizations since opportunities for such pitfalls are plentiful. "No cop-outs" emphasizes to residents the need to free themselves from the past, to live "one day at a time," to act responsibly at this moment, not to think about previous failures, or worry about tomorrow. Discouraging cop-outs and encouraging residents to view themselves (not drugs) as the problem in a positive and constructive way leads them into an active involvement in their own therapy and fosters responsibility in others not to cop-out.

Act As If

Changing the self-talk from negatives to positive does not occur in a vacuum. It must be supplemented and reinforced with appropriate behavior patterns and these are fostered by the colloquialism, "act as if." To "act as if" means to (1) set positive behavioral goals and standards, (2) continue to repeat positive, self-enhancing statements about yourself and your potential, and (3) behave as if you are and have these positive characteristics.

"Acting as if" is based on the belief that we *are* as we behave. Self-thoughts and behaviors required of the resident are carefully specified and agreed to by the resident, peers, and staff. The basic premise underlying this approach is similar to that involved in the socialization of the child. Patterns of behavior and effective styles of coping not currently part of the behavioral repertoire need to be learned or relearned. As this repertoire expands, so do choices.

One type of behavior that is always required is to *act responsibly.* Responsibility is defined in terms of personal hygiene, cooperation in work assignments, and the display of courtesy and concern toward peers.

Residents experience rewards for their new and positive behaviors, initially from other residents and staff, but eventually from themselves as the process becomes self-reinforcing. By acting positively they begin to think and feel better about themselves. "Pull-ups," pointing out behavioral and thinking errors, occur when a resident fails to "act as if." However, the emphasis is on rewarding appropriate behavior rather than focusing on mistakes.

In brief, residents decide what they want to be, act as if they already are that way, and are rewarded for it. In time, they come to think of themselves as being that way and act as they want to be.

Turnaround

The colloquialism "turnaround" refers to two behavioral objectives: (1) the *personal* turnaround in which residents define their own goals in life in terms of their beliefs, and (2) the *other-oriented* turnaround in which residents serve as a positive role model, helping other members of the community achieve their objectives.

Psychological well-being is a product of beliefs about oneself and the world in which one lives. Those who believe themselves to be pawns of forces beyond their control will likely drift and display little initiative. Those who perceive others to be of little worth will ignore peoples' feelings and manipulate them for personal benefit.

The personal turnaround initially involves a process of

self-scrutiny and an examination of basic beliefs and personal goals in life and ultimately a decision to defend those ideals and subject them to public scrutiny.

The other-oriented turnaround goes to the heart of the therapeutic community and involves the resident looking beyond the self and learning to listen to, care about, and help other persons (cf. Glaser, 1976). Each resident has the responsibility for serving as a positive role model for others. In Synanon's jargon, this is *walking the talk.*

To turn around is to give to others successfully what one has received: "putting something back into the pot." It should occur throughout residency and increase with seniority. The *ultimate* turnaround involves graduates of the program staying on as ex-addict staff members. Becoming an ex-addict staff member at *414* was only *one* of the options available for those who successfully completed the reentry phase. The ultimate turnaround may also involve putting back into society by becoming straight, getting a job, and staying away from drugs and crime.

No Free Lunch

No cop-outs, act as if, and turnaround are reinforced by a fourth colloquialism, "no free lunch." Within the therapeutic community, residents are held responsible for their own personal growth and for contributing to an atmosphere that will help others grow. When a resident gives up or takes an "I don't care" or "I don't want to change" attitude, that person is not only interfering with his or her own rehabilitation but with that of the entire family. Such a person is seen as sucking the therapeutic marrow from the collective bones of the community and becomes a parasitic free lunch seeker. "No free lunch" constantly challenges residents to do their share and, if necessary, more than their share to become self-reliant, to accept what they earned through their efforts, and to expect no more from life than what they put into it.

GAMES

The game is a form of encounter group therapy developed at Synanon (Casriel, 1963; Volkman & Cressey, 1963; Yablonsky, 1965; Endore, 1968). It is an intense forum for personal learning and development. Games are emotional free-for-alls that carry with them the belief and expectation that personal emotional growth comes from honesty. Participants are forced to examine critically both the positive and negative aspects of themselves and others and to share their observations and feelings with members of the group (Yablonsky, 1965). As Casriel (1963) puts it, "each member is a therapist and each therapist is a member."

The Purpose of the Game

The purpose of the game is to challenge the residents to explore and discover the real and valuable parts of their lives and to grow in the midst of candid interpersonal scrutiny. The therapeutic community provides a protected environment within which to make these efforts. The operative premise is that members who participate fully in the game develop greater respect for themselves and others and begin to move toward living self-reliant and responsible lives.

The Rules of the Game

The cardinal rule of the game is simple: no physical violence. Feelings can be expressed in any language at any volume, but members are aware that this freedom is restricted to the game and behavior that is acceptable in the game is not necessarily acceptable outside of the encounter.

Another norm is to "leave your garbage in the room." It is considered destructive to carry bad feelings out of the game and into the family. Residents feel more comfortable challenging each other in the game situation, knowing that it will be discussed only in this context with no repercussions outside the game. Another rule is that contracts or agreements that may be made between members—for instance, to protect each other—must be broken during the game.

The Form of the Game

Games start promptly at a prearranged time with participants sitting in a circle, a seating arrangement that maximizes closeness and facilitates emotional and behavioral encounters. Furniture, pictures, and drapes are removed to reduce distractions and help participants concentrate.

In some therapeutic communities such as Daytop (Bassin, 1974) and Synanon (Yablonsky, 1965), the membership of each new game changes in order to reduce the likelihood that members contract to "gang up on" or "to go easy on" each other. *414* games were organized in terms of the level of residents. For instance, probationary residents participated in one game, reentry residents in another. Occasionally, "salt-and-pepper" games were held with members drawn from all levels. These games allowed older residents to get to know the newer members or to teach the new members skills to be taken back to their own game.

Special games called to deal with emergency situations such as someone considering splitting were "games of the whole," in which all residents participated. Marathon games (also "games of the whole") lasting for several days were called to deal with serious problems requiring remedial action, such as declining morale in the house. These games would be interrupted by common consent for a few hours sleep, or to excuse a member to prepare meals.

The Role of the Expediter

One member of the group, designated as the expediter, is responsible for the pace and tone of the game but does not function as a group leader in the same sense as the therapist in traditional group psychotherapy. The expediter is, foremost, a member of the group and as such is open to the criticism of others. The expediter has achieved, rather than ascribed, authority and is chosen largely as a function of his or her experience as a skilled game player. The expediter keeps the game on track, insuring that each participant is scrutinized at some point during the session by commenting on that person's mood, behavior, or silence. In the early games at *414,* senior staff members served as expediters. When residents became more skilled they took on this role

The Process of the Game.

Considerable tension and anxiety is attendant to game playing regardless of the level of experience of the players. Group members experience a conflict between the excitement and challenge of learning and growing and the fear of the hard, painful work necessary to accomplish this. Caught between the values of positive change and the preservation of the status quo, it often appears safer to be secretive, to hold on to pretenses, to resist self-examination, openness, and honesty in the group. The risks involved in self-disclosure appear too great. The resolution of this conflict, faced by each participant each time, is the essence of the successful game. With experience the opportunity to express beliefs becomes exhilarating and begins to outweigh fear.

The process of the game involves making specific indictments of a participant sometimes called "pulling covers." This means being exposed, having basic values challenged, or behavioral lapses announced to the group. A member may employ many techniques to counter an indictment by other participants and might minimize the incident or deny the accusation. Denials are typically countered with additional evidence until the participant capitulates, admits the error, and begins to examine his or her behavior more closely.

A "motion," or behavioral prescription, is usually given to the person successfully indicted. It is tailored to alter the indicted person's behavior. Motions, such as doing extra work, are arrived at through group concensus and have the individual's support. These contracts are reassessed, continued, or adjusted at the next game depending on circumstances and the person's progress.

Participants sometimes come to the aid of a fellow resident who is on the "hot seat." Such interventions are usually defined as false rescues and frequently lead to an indictment of the rescuer for not having enough faith in the other resident's ability to stand up for himself or herself. Each resident has to learn both to rely on his or her own resources and to allow others to be self-reliant.

Through the process of confrontation, indictment, and motion the residents are forced to discover, define, and defend themselves. By examining who they are and what they are doing, feelings and behaviors are brought to the surface where they can be scrutinized.

Confrontation occurs in a highly emotional atmosphere that is not so much threatening as it is supportive and allows participants to experience a broad range of human emotions. The mood of the game can change quickly and dramatically, from one of deep despair to one of supportive uncontrolled hilarity. The sounds from the game room are loud: shouting, screaming, crying, and laughing can be heard at some time during almost every game. At times, however, there is no sound as participants in the game share a feeling, touching one another emotionally in silent community.

Reentry Games

Games composed entirely of reentry candidates deal with more intellectual and philosophical topics related to problems of living in the outside world. Occasionally, these games deal with practical matters such as learning to complete application forms for jobs. However, at *414* and other therapeutic communities (cf. Bassin, 1974) the games tended to focus on values and personality weaknesses.

At *414,* as with the programs at Phoenix and Odyssey, residents had additional opportunities: individual counseling and special group sessions were organized in order to promote personal growth. A special group for females dealt with problems of self-concept; enrichment groups employed techniques of bioenergetics, dance, relaxation, and music therapy; seminars held twice a week and mealtime readings facilitated cultural and educational enrichment.

Staff Participation in the Game

Staff members are also subject to confrontations in the game and are not given preferential treatment. They receive indictments for being negative, for not giving of themselves, and for pulling rank by asserting ascribed authority. Their performance in dealing with these indictments is highly visible to the residents and provides role modeling. When a staff member learns and grows as a result of the game, so do the residents.

Criticisms of the Game

Criticisms of the game generally fall into three areas (cf. Colburn & Colburn, 1973; Mahon, 1973; Rachman & Heller, 1974). First, the game is criticized as dehumanizing, demanding subjugation of individual to the group, often with no rational basis (Colburn & Colburn, 1973; Malcolm, 1973b). Second, the honest and confronting style of the successful game player is criticized as unsuited for living in the world outside of the therapeutic community (Mahon, 1973). Brewster and Garrigues (1974) argue that the game serves its purpose best in a residential setting and they caution against the "square games" run by Synanon for nonresident nonaddicts. Third, critics express the fear that the intense emotional and psychological pressure of the game may precipitate psychotic breaks in vulnerable individuals (Colburn & Colburn, 1973; Patalano, 1976).

Evidence neither supports nor refutes these objections. Some perspectives can be offered, however, to partly counter these arguments. The candid, attacking, profane style of expressing emotions in the game is as inappropriate for the family life in the therapeutic community outside of the game as it is for the outside world. The therapeutic community acknowledges a responsibility for preparing residents to identify and understand what is appropriate in different contexts. Part of the function of reentry groups is to train respondents to successfully control their emotional response without sacrificing the experience of self-examination.

Unfair criticism of a group member stemming from projection or hostility on the part of the attacker is frequently identified and corrected by other group members. The game does involve stripping away protective masks, but it also provides reinforcement for real and genuine self-expression. Members discover what they do not like and what they prize about themselves and others. Expediters insure that an individual who is taken apart is put back together again. Such encounters appear to be better suited to a residential setting, which guarantees physical, social, and emotional support outside of the game, than to an outpatient setting.

Casriel (1972) and Brewster and Garrigues (1974) caution against the treatment of overt psychosis in encounter groups. However, Casriel (1972) indicates that few drug addicts are actually psychotic. The majority are diagnosed as having character disorders, and these people are likely to become good game players and benefit from the experience. Brewster and Garrigues (1974) additionally caution that the game ought not to be played by novices without the assistance of a skilled game player, nor should games be played outside the residential setting.

Critics of the encounter group tend to focus on the process of the game rather than on its purpose. The game may appear brutal to an outsider, but it facilitates direct, honest self-examination, and it challenges the participants to explore their values, beliefs, and behaviors so as to achieve a well-grounded self-concept.

Conclusions

The purpose of the therapeutic community is to produce individuals who are able to cope with their feelings and their environment. Core components of this milieu are expressed in the colloquialisms and the game. The colloquialisms constitute articulations of the principles on which life in the community and its therapeutic component are based. Persons must accept responsibility for their problems and not blame others (no cop-out); they must behave as they believe they should even though this behavior is not yet congruent with how they feel that they actually are (act as if); members must take responsibility for their own treatment and that of others (no free lunch); and residents must serve as a positive role model for others (turn-around).

The game or encounter is a key part of the therapeutic community. It is a forum for emotional interchange and growth and fosters honesty of expression and self-examination. However, in the absence of skilled and responsible game players, games may be dangerous in a residential setting.

Chapter 3

METHODOLOGY: DESIGN FOR EVALUATION

Available information on the effectiveness of the therapeutic community in treating drug-dependent persons tends to be anecdotal, testimonial, and colored by hopes of success. The limited information on the effectiveness of therapeutic communities, both past and present, can be accounted for by several factors. First, while such approaches to treatment have been extant for about 20 years, most communities were started with the sole objective of delivering a service. Systematic research and evaluation has been seen as a task that is low on the scale of priorities. Second, it has been, at times, eschewed as a meaningless activity that might detract from the real job at hand—treatment. Cruskey and Krasner (1973) put it this way:

> "therapeutic communities" . . . including Gaudenzia House, Daytop Village, Phoenix House and a variety of others [have had] . . . highly publicized and enthusiastic successes . . . . They rely heavily on faith, exhortation and on being remade from the inside out, and tend to be antagonistic toward academic expertise and all its statistical works.

Third, a willingness to *believe* that the therapeutic community works on the basis of limited or questionable evidence may well stem from our despair about what to do with chemically dependent persons, especially heroin addicts.[1] Yablonsky's (1965) book on Synanon has frequently been cited to support the therapeutic community approach. However, much of that evidence is testimonial or impressionistic in character and does not allow firm conclusions about the efficacy or efficiency of Synanon in the treatment of heroin addicts.

The potential value of the therapeutic community in the treatment of chemically dependent persons has been mentioned frequently (e.g., Boorstein, 1967; Deissler, 1970; Popour, 1972; Le Dain, 1972; Whitehead & Brook, 1973; Knox, 1974; Charuvastra & Charbeneaux, 1977). Advocates remain convinced that drug addiction can be effectively treated in such an environment (Rosenthal & Baise, 1969; Waldorf, 1971; Kaufman & De Leon, 1978) and it is not uncommon to find in their rhetoric mention of rates of success as high as 60 or 70%. On the other hand, Cohen (1974) believes that therapeutic communities only attract about 2% of the chemically dependent population. Consequently, even if such high rates of success do obtain, and it is doubtful that they do, the total number of persons assisted by the method must be low indeed.

The special advantage of the therapeutic community is seen to be in its emphasis on the peer structure, environmental control and immediate reinforcement, and sanctions that are perceived to offset the immaturity, ego deficits, and lack of socialization generally found in chemically dependent persons.

Some writers use single case studies, clinical impressions (e.g., Casriel, 1963; Yablonsky, 1971), or highly selected samples of clients as the empirical basis for conclusions about the success of the therapeutic community (Brill, 1971). Many judgments are not based on analyses of reliable data (LeDain, 1973). Reports of systematic research have focused on the treatment process rather than outcome. Prosocial changes such as a decrease in criminal behavior and a reduction in drug-using behavior seem to occur as a function of long-term and continued residence within a therapeutic community (De Leon, et al., 1972; De Leon et al. 1973). Gold and Coghlan (1973), report positive changes in self-esteem and appropriate internalization of control as a function of residence within the therapeutic community. However, to conclude from these data that therapeutic communities are successful is questionable on at least three counts: (1) the data generally do not take into account the high numbers of people who drop out of the program; (2) it is not clear that such changes can be attributed to treatment; and (3) it is not clear that changes are sustained when residents return to the larger society.

It is increasingly evident that graduates of therapeutic communities are few and far between (Collier, 1973a). The few systematic follow-up studies that are available indicate that dropouts and even graduates from the program have a high incidence of relapse (Stephens & Cottrell, 1972; Brill, 1971). Without reliable data or systematic and carefully documented follow-up studies, the efficacy of therapeutic communities as a treatment modality cannot be assessed with any degree of accuracy.

From its inception, *414* was unique among therapeutic communities on two major counts. First, it was the only therapeutic community established specifically for the treatment of amphetamine abusers. Second, it was established as a demonstration project and was commited to systematically researching the efficacy of the therapeutic community program. This commitment and the integration of a research component into the program made it possible to collect information on both the residents and the program on a prospective basis. Program decisions were not always made in terms of what was best for the research design (see, for example, Brook, 1975), but the presence of a research orientation allowed for a program that could be—and was—evaluated.

Original planning of the evaluation considered the use of an independent control group of persons not treated at *414* to be compared with *414* residents. This plan anticipated two conditions: first, that more persons would seek treatment than could be admitted, thus allowing the use of the "waiting list" technique to form a control group (cf. Campbell & Stanley, 1963). Second, a sufficient number of persons would seek alternative types of treatment (e.g., as outpatient) and could be used as a comparison group. These conditions never prevailed.

Few young people sought admission and at the beginning our objective was to have at least 15 residents at a time, since this would allow for a reasonably broad range of residents who could serve as role models for one another. This was difficult to achieve even by admitting all comers. Thus, during the early period a waiting list was a luxury we could not afford.

The optimum—and near maximum—capacity of *414* of between 20 and 25 residents was reached after the first few months, and was maintained reasonably well over the next 12 to 18 months. Except for one brief period, there was never an excess of people seeking residence. During the exceptional period a peak of 35 residents caused the capacity of the facility to be stretched. In the fall of 1973, the number of residents and potential admissions began to decline.

The use of alternative client populations from the community did not prove to be an option in establishing an appropriate comparison group. Persons seen in outpatient treatment or at the special drug units at local hospitals (general and psychiatric) were at some point invariably referred to *414* because it was part of the Network of Treatment Services. The inability to generate an independent control group has been characterized by the LeDain Commission as a hazard that is endemic to this type of research:

> It is doubtful if there can ever be satisfactory comparative evaluation of the results achieved by the therapeutic community and other forms of treatment or management. Apart from a difference of goals in many cases, there is the difficulty of establishing suitably matched control groups (LeDain, 1973).

Our research addresses itself to the question of whether participating in a therapeutic community results in people being better adjusted behaviorally or psychologically than would have been the case if these people had not been exposed to the therapeutic community. Due to the absence of a true experimental design causality cannot be inferred. However, the presence or absence of fairly strong correlational evidence can determine whether treatment is associated with improved functioning.

Design

The type of design chosen for this evaluation is longitudinal with repeated measures. First, residents were tested three times: once when they entered *414* and twice after they left the community allowing for pre-post comparisons. Second, the use of a sequential follow-up design allowed for the interval of time between departure from *414* and first posttest to be the same for all residents. This allows the correlation between time spent in treatment and condition at follow-up to be measured, while controlling for (by holding constant) time away from *414*.

One of the difficult issues involved in assessing the impact of treatment is determining the amount of treatment received by each individual exposed to it. The fact that the treatment is part of the social environment to which each individual contributes and from which each individual draws does not mean that each person will respond equally to a given amount of exposure to treatment. A completely satisfactory solution for measuring the amount of treatment people receive in therapeutic communities has not been identified.

The most common solution that has been utilized has been to use exposure to treatment as a proxy for the amount of treatment one has received. *Time in treatment*—usually called *time in program*—has been used as the measure of treatment received in attempts to assess various aspects of therapeutic communities (Volkman & Cressey, 1963; Rohrs et al., 1971; De Leon et al., 1972; De Leon, 1973; Lesser, 1974; Collier & Hijazi, 1974; De Leon, 1978; De Leon & Andrews, 1977; NIDA, 1977; Kaufman & De Leon, 1978; Holland, 1978). These studies analyze data on time in program in terms of categories of length of stay. Even studies by the same author do not use the same boundaries for these categories and there is no systematic definition of them. In our own work, we have found that "results" are considerably different when boundaries of time in treatment categories are altered and that there is no intrinsic solution to the question of which boundaries are appropriate. It is for these reasons that we have come to decide that time in treatment is best treated as a continuous variable—number of days in residence (which also has the advantage of forming a ratio scale)—rather than one that is arbitrarily divided into gross categories of length of stay. The measure is quantitative and does not involve a qualitative assessment of the treatment to which residents are exposed.

In order to measure qualitative aspects of exposure to treatment an additional variable was utilized in this study: the highest level achieved by each resident while in the therapeutic community. Promotion from one level to another is a function of the judgments made by peers and staff concerning one's performance in the therapeutic community and, as such, presumably indicates the impact of treatment. However, time in treatment and highest level achieved are so highly correlated ($r = .90$) as to preclude the use of both variables; thus days in treatment was chosen because it forms a ratio scale with a broad range, from 1 day to 534 days.

In summary, the study was designed to investigate the relevance of the length of time spent in treatment for behavioral and psychological adjustment at two follow-up periods.

SUBJECTS

A total of 156 persons was admitted to *414* during its existence. Some stayed an hour or two, others stayed well over a year. Only fragmentary information could be obtained on some of these persons before they left. Some items in the documentation may have been lost through clerical errors. Consequently, there are complete admission data on 117 persons. However, missing information is more characteristic of people who entered the program during its earliest days rather than those who were admitted during the period covered by our follow-up study. The follow-up was designed to reach all residents who had been in treatment at *414* on March 1, 1972 or who were admitted to the program between that date and February 28, 1973. Seventy-four residents, constituting 47% of all persons ever admitted to *414*, and 63% of persons on whom there were admission data fell into this category. Based on the comparisons that we have been able to make, the persons followed-up are representative of all admissions. This feature of the follow-up design is relatively unique among evaluations of therapeutic communities, in that unlike other studies no selection factor was used to include or exclude particular individuals, on the basis of status, graduation, or length of time in the program.

Former residents were first followed-up 10 months after they left *414*. Seventy-one of the 74 persons (96%) were successfully recontacted and interviewed. Three could not be recontacted, 6 of the 71 successful recontacts were not retested because they were uncooperative, psychologically unable to participate, or were evading the police. Therefore, complete follow-up information is available on 65 (88%) of the persons designated for follow-up.

The second follow-up was conducted in 1976, approximately 4 years after the residents left *414.* Among those who completed the first follow-up, 57 (88%) were successfully followed-up a second time. Of the 57 former residents who were located, 2 refused to be tested. Three were partially tested, but did not complete the MMPI, and the MMPI of another person was considered invalid.

This study involves a follow-up of 55 former residents for whom there were pretreatment and follow-up data (except for test scores on the MMPI that are based on 51 persons). These 55 residents constitute 74% of the persons in the original follow-up design.

Instruments

Three instruments were used to collect information on former residents at follow-up: a face sheet completed at the time of entry at *414,* the Minnesota Multiphasic Personality Inventory (MMPI), and a special questionnaire used at the time of follow-up.

Additional sources of information were included to provide a more complete portrait of the residents. For instance, we obtained the academic records of some residents and IQ tests were administered in some cases. A small study was also conducted that involved sending a questionnaire to the parents of the residents (cf. Brook et al., 1976). This questionnaire examined the temporal relationship between a variety of psychosocial problems that young people may have encountered and their drug-abusing behaviors. The questionnaire was sent to the parents of all the 117 residents on whom there was complete information: 50% (59) were returned completed, 33% (39) were not returned, 15% (17) were returned "address unknown," and 2% (2) were returned incomplete.

Face Sheet and Follow-up Questionnaires.

People who were admitted to treatment completed a face sheet that included information on age, sex, religious affiliation, occupation of father, religion of parents, scholastic history, work history, previous psychological or psychiatric counseling as an in-patient or out-patient, history of drug use, residential mobility, marital status, living arrangements, and legal involvements. Similar information was collected at the time of each follow-up.

A few of these items were selected to form a single measure of behavioral functioning. Chambers and Inciardi (1974) developed an index of successful outcome based on three criteria: employment, involvement with the criminal justice system, and use of drugs. In this analysis these criteria are operationalized in the following manner. Former residents who were in school or working regularly (two-thirds of the time) during the 10 months prior to the first follow-up and 12 months prior to the second follow-up are considered to have met the criterion of employment. Those who report no arrests or incarcerations during the 10- and 12-month periods prior to follow-up meet the criterion related to police involvement. The criterion of success for drug use is met by abstinence from the use of all drugs (except marihuana or alcohol) at the time of the follow-up interview and abstinence from the use of opiates and amphetamines since leaving the therapeutic community. In keeping with Chambers and Inciardi (1974), former residents who meet all three criteria are referred to as "completely successful"; those who meet two of the criteria are "partially successful"; and those who only meet one criterion or who fail to meet any of the criteria are "failures."

The MMPI

The basic measure of psychological status used at *414* is the Minnesota Multiphasic Personality Inventory (Form R). Many reference texts describe the instrument in detail as well as its use and interpretations (cf. Dahlstrom, Welsh, & Dahlstrom, 1975; Lachar, 1974; Marks, Seeman, & Haller, 1974).

The MMPI, a self-administered psychological test, consists of 566 true-false items. It was originally designed as an objective psychometric instrument for diagnostic purposes. The

MMPI contains 10 clinical scales, each of which has a name relating it to a specific psychodiagnostic category.[2]

During the 30 years that the MMPI has been in use it has been determined that the actual content and meaning of each scale, relative to the diagnostic label by which each is identified, is limiting and unclear in interpreting and communicating findings. The scales are now commonly referred to by their numbers rather than by the diagnostic labels.

The MMPI was administered on admission, at the 10-month follow-up, and at the 4-year follow-up. Theoretically, scores (called T-scores) above 70 indicate psychological maladjustment while T-scores between 50 and 70 represent the range of normality. Over the years, inconsistencies between clinical diagnoses and the results of MMPI tests have led to interpretations based on the elevations of the clinical scales relative to one another. These, known as high point codes, provide a more complete personality assessment than can be obtained from examining each of the scales separately. Various patterns of scale elevation have been identified and have repeatedly been found to describe certain types of individuals.

It is customary to convert raw scores to age-specific standard scores (T-scores) when comparisons between groups are to be made. But insofar as this analysis is not concerned with comparisons across groups, raw scores are employed to obtain an index of psychological functioning for a single group at multiple points in time. Given that at first testing residents were in their late adolescence and by the third testing they were young adults, the use of raw scores also precludes any confusion as to whether "adolescent" or "adult" norms are appropriate and allows for more straightforward analysis across time periods for the same sample. However, sex differences are not corrected for by the use of raw scores. Consequently, age-appropriate T-score conversions were made when testing for differences between males and females.

Most readers will not be interested in the technical details so the results of this testing are presented largely in an interpreted form.[3]

Procedures

Residents were interviewed and completed the psychological tests shortly after arriving at *414*. Testing was delayed for those who were toxic on admission.

Two waves of follow-up of our former residents were conducted, 10 months and 4 years after termination of treatment. The time between termination of treatment and the first follow-up was constant for all residents, but the interval between termination of treatment and 4-year follow-up was not precisely the same in all cases. For practical purposes the variation of a few months over a period of 48 months is probably of little importance.

Because of these features, the possible effects of *time in treatment* on the residents' posttreatment functioning can be assessed. Campbell and Stanley (1963) consider this approach to be appropriate where the various treatment groups are undifferentiated on important dependent variables at pretest, a situation that obtains in this study.

Longitudinal designs are generally considered superior to others, since they permit the study of cause and effect relationships between variables, an advantage that is not obtained with cross-sectional analysis (Svalastoga, 1970). However, certain disadvantages that accompany research conducted over time frequently discourage potential users. This type of research is usually costly, time consuming, and presents problems in maintaining contact with persons who are mobile (Eckland, 1968; see Ball, 1972, for a discussion of successful follow-up studies).

Procedures were adopted to overcome such difficulties. In order to minimize the number of persons lost to follow-up, the technique of personal interviews was adopted. This technique has yielded higher rates of returns than either telephone calls or mailings (Crider, Willits, & Bealer, 1971). It was also recognized that former residents had to be sought out personally and not simply invited to return for an interview.

Dedication and perseverance are some of the crucial factors that contribute to following up a large proportion of cases successfully. A success rate of 100% was achieved during the early months of the first follow-up. It was a positive reinforcement and fostered a high level of motivation among the fieldworkers who were trying to reach hard-to-contact persons.

The average amount of time needed to follow-up each case was 8 hours. This varied from a sucession of 18-hour days needed to track down a single person to the good fortune of locating and testing three or four persons during a single day. About 50% of the former residents were located during evenings and weekends.

Various resources were utilized to establish the residents' current whereabouts. Twenty-three (35%) parents responding to our questionnaire supplied information as to current addresses of former residents. Other sources of such information were creditors, employers, and friends of the residents. In most cases, a combination of resources was accessed either by telephone or in-person.

The follow-up workers pursued available leads and tried to reach the residents at their most recent address. If they no longer lived there, the resident's neighbors were questioned and more information was sought. If the resident had moved to another community and leads were exhausted, staff members at social service agencies were contacted. In cases where this failed —a not-infrequent occurrence—follow-up workers would go to the residents' known hangouts such as pool halls, taverns, and street corners and simply wait for the resident to arrive. Once the former resident was located, payment of $10 was offered as an incentive for those who refused to particpate at first. This applied to only 10 to 15% of all cases.

Several of the former residents located in this manner were still in London, the majority were out of town, although still in Ontario, and a few were located and tested in other provinces (such as Quebec and British Columbia). Approximately one-half of the residents were tested in their own homes, while others were interviewed at local Addiction Research Foundation clinics or in institutional settings (prisons and hospitals), and the remaining in libraries, cars, parks, office buildings, or wherever there was room.

About one-half of those tested at the Addiction Research Foundation were tested on a group basis. All others, however, were tested individually, in separate rooms, with the assistance of the follow-up workers. Since a follow-up worker typically spent a good deal of time talking with the ex-resident before raising the question of completing the follow-up documentation, it is likely that many perceived the follow-up contact as an opportunity to meet someone who demonstrated personal concern for their welfare, rather than as a request to give something to science. Information from completed forms and interviews was validated by contacting family, friends, employers, or schools of the former resident where applicable. Police files were also checked and a thorough computer search for each resident was provided by the federal parole board and local police authorities. We did not find evidence of invalidity and this is consistent with the findings of Ogborne and Melotte's (1977) follow-up of therapeutic community residents in England.

The data were coded, key punched, verified, and analyzed by computer. Tests of significance on demographic data were conducted with the chi-square technique. T-tests were employed to assess differences on the MMPI scales. One-way analysis of covariance techniques was employed to test for the effects of (1) background variables and (2) supplementary treatment on outcome status. Time in treatment is the covariate in this analysis. Pearson zero-order correlations are the principal statistical test used for assessing the effects of treatment. Correlations were calculated among the variables: days in treatment, scores of the Chambers and Inciardi Index, and scores for all scales of the MMPI. Unless otherwise indicated the criterion of statistical significance utilized is the .05 level.

Representativeness of the Follow-up Sample

In order to generalize beyond the sample, it is necessary to compare the residents in the follow-up sample ($N = 55$) with other residents of *414* on whom there are complete data ($N = 62$) in terms of characteristics considered to be programmatically relevant. (With respect to analysis of MMPI data, 51 residents from the follow-up sample are compared to the other 65 residents.)

An examination of background characteristics reveals only a few statistically significant differences between residents followed-up and those not followed-up (Table 3.1). Residents who were followed up had (1) a higher grade average, (2) repeated more grades, (3) been in the drug scene longer, and (4) made fewer attempts at suicide than those who were not followed up. The two groups were not different in terms of age, sex, religious affiliation, religion of father, religion of mother, residential mobility, father's occupation, parents' marital status, number of siblings, birth order, last grade completed in school, type of academic program, drug of choice, previous drug-related treatment, previous psychiatric treatment, and previous involvement with the court. Therefore, there were few differences in background characteristics between residents followed up and those who were not.

These two groups were also compared in terms of psychological characteristics on admission to *414* (Figure 3.1). The shape, slope, and elevation of the composite MMPI profile indicates psychological disturbance characterized by fractured and disoriented thought patterns with paranoid features, agitation, depression, pronounced mood swings, social isolation, and withdrawal with tendencies toward sociopathy. These common psychological features are more dominant than the measured differences between the residents followed up and those not followed up.

Statistical differences between these groups are evident on four clinical scales and the validity scale F. The follow-up

Table 3.1 Background Information on Residents of 414 Who Are in the Follow-up Sample (N = 55) and Those Who Are Not (N = 69)

	414 Follow-up Sample (N=*55*)		*414 Residents* (N = *69*)		
	N	*Percent*	N	*Percent*	χ^2
Sex					
males	41	74.5	51	73.9	
females	14	25.5	18	26.1	.02
Mean age					
$\bar{x}$ age	19.6		20		
Religion					
Protestant	37	68.5	42	62.0	
Catholic	16	29.6	24	35.3	
Other	—		1	1.5	
None	1	1.9	1	1.5	2.12
Religion of father					
Protestant	37	80.4	36	65.5	
Catholic	9	19.5	18	32.7	
Other	—	—	1	1.8	3.57
Religion of mother					
Protestant	37	74.0	37	66.1	
Catholic	13	26.0	18	32.1	
Other	—	—	1	1.8	3.83
Residences					
1	—		2	3.1	
2	6	11.8	—	—	
3	4	7.8	7	10.8	
4	9	17.6	7	10.8	
5	8	15.7	9	13.8	
5+	24	47.1	40	61.5	13.34
Father's occupation					
Professional	6	11.8	9	13.4	
Proprietor	6	11.8	7	10.4	
Clerical/sales	3	5.9	4	6.0	
Skilled	16	31.4	17	25.4	
Semiskilled	14	27.5	12	17.9	
None/deceased	6	17.8	18	26.9	6.17

Table 3.1 Continued

	414 Follow-up Sample (N=55)		*414 Residents (N = 69)*		
	N	*Percent*	N	*Percent*	χ^2
Parents' marital status					
Married	37	69.8	37	54.4	
Divorced/separated	11	20.7	13	19.1	
One parent deceased	4	7.5	14	20.6	
Both deceased	1	1.9	4	5.9	7.21
Number of siblings					
0	4	7.7	4	6.8	
1	9	17.3	17	28.8	
2	8	15.4	11	18.6	
3	14	26.9	10	16.9	
3+	17	32.7	17	28.8	6.18
Birth order					
1st	15	28.8	20	34.5	
2nd	18	34.6	26	44.8	
3rd	11	21.2	6	10.3	
More than 3rd	8	15.4	6	10.3	9.15
Last grade completed					
Less than grade 8	15	27.8	10	14.7	
Grade 9–10	19	35.2	39	57.4	
Grade 11–12	17	31.5	14	20.6	
Grade 13	—	—	2	2.9	
Post high school	3	5.6	3	4.4	13.05
Grades repeated					
0	12	23.5	18	34.6	
1	22	43.1	20	38.5	
2+	17	33.3	14	26.9	8.16*
Academic program					
Technical	14	27.4	21	33.9	
College preparatory	19	37.2	24	38.7	
Special/vocational	18	35.3	17	27.4	1.26
Grade average					
Less than 50%	—	—	1	2.3	
50–59	7	14.9	8	18.2	
60–69	24	51.1	24	54.5	
70–79	9	19.1	9	20.5	
80+	7	14.9	2	4.5	18.52*

Table 3.1 Continued

	414 Follow-up Sample (N=55)		*414 Residents (N = 69)*		
	N	*Percent*	N	*Percent*	χ^2
Duration heavy drug use					
Less than 6 months	—	—	1	2.3	
6 mo.–1 yr.	11	20.7	15	21.7	
1–2 yrs.	8	15.1	22	31.9	
2–3 yrs.	8	15.1	10	14.5	
3+ yrs.	26	49.1	19	27.5	10.79*
Drug of choice					
Hallucinogens	7	13.0	10	14.5	
Amphetamines	35	64.8	45	65.2	
Opiates	10	18.5	13	18.8	
Other	2	3.8	1	1.4	1.36
Previous treatment (drug related)	46	85.2	53	76.8	1.82
Previous treatment (psychiatric)	35	64.8	43	62.3	.82
Suicide attempts	25	46.3	40	58.0	6.02*
Court involvements					
None	12	23.5	19	27.9	
Drug related	5	9.8	6	8.8	
Nondrug related	23	45.1	32	47.1	
Both	11	21.6	11	16.2	3.41

*Significance level, $P < .05$.

sample displayed less in the way of neurotic patterns associated with abnormal concern for body functions, less use of physical symptoms to solve conflict and avoid responsibility, less disregard for social custom and mores, and less paranoia. However, from a clinical and interpretive point of view, these differences are minimal. The profile elevation of the follow-up sample is three standard deviations above the mean, and within the range of serious pathology. Where scale differences occur they neither alter the pattern of the profile nor do they suggest differential psychopathology.

In brief, the following features characterize this study: a high proportion of former residents in the sample to be followed up were successfully reinterviewed and retested during two follow-up periods; those successfully followed-up are in general undifferentiated from former residents who were not followed-up. This means that the results are not apt to be biased as a result of factors of selection in the process of follow-up and the results are generalizable to all residents of *414*. Rusee, McBride, McCoy, and Inciardi (Hill, 1976) indicate that such generalizability is rare in follow-up studies of former residents of treatment programs.

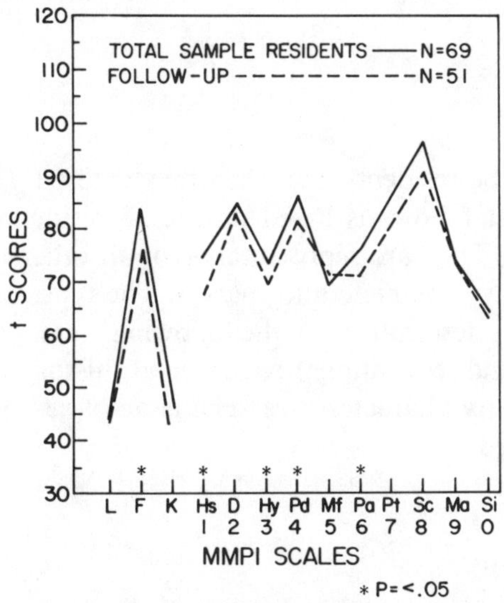

Fig. 3.1 Composite MMPL Profile for Follow-up Sample and Residents of 414

Chapter 4

RESIDENTS OF *414*: THE WAY THEY WERE

What were the residents like when they entered *414*? The description that follows is based on the 55 residents who were followed up. They are representative of all other residents on whom we have complete information. The types of items that comprise this description are the following: demographic, family background, educational background, history of drug use, and personality characteristics. The issue of sex differences is also examined.

Demographic

Sex

Most (75%) of the residents of *414* were male. This 3:1 ratio of drug abusers characterizes the sex ratio in other therapeutic communities (Nash, Waldorf, Foster, & Kyllingstad, 1974).

Age

414 residents ranged from 15 to 25 years of age with an average of nearly 20 years. They tended to be younger than at other therapeutic communities for two reasons. First, *414* was established specifically for adolescents, which is uncommon, and second, the drug of choice is amphetamines, which tends to be associated with young persons.

Marital Status

Ninety-six percent of the residents were unmarried when they came to *414*. Four percent, all females, were either separated or divorced from their partners. Two of the female residents had a child who resided with their parents. They had no contact with their children while in residence.

Religion

Two-thirds of the residents were Protestant, 30% were Catholic, and a small minority expressed no religious preference. There tended to be a high level of agreement between the religious preference of residents and their parents. In general, they were not practicing members of a church or synagogue and their attendance at services was infrequent.

Residential Mobility

The residents of *414* were characterized by high rates of residential mobility with a mean number of 6.4 residences, many reporting 9 or more residences since birth. The majority of these residential changes occurred subsequent to involvement with illicit drugs. Few of the residents lived with their parents prior to admission. Most lived alone or with drug-using friends.

Family Background

Age of Parents

The mean age of fathers of entering residents was 50 years and of their mothers 46 years.

Religion of Parents

The religious affiliations of the parents were similar to the residents themselves, the majority reported to be Protestants. A very small proportion reported no religious preference.

Occupation of Father

Broad categories were used to classify the occupation of the fathers of the residents. These categories include professional or managerial, proprietors of small businesses, clerical and sales, skilled or technical trades, and semiskilled trades. In addition, a category for unemployed and deceased was included. About 12% of the fathers fell into the latter category. Thirty-one percent were employed in skilled trades, 27% in semiskilled, 6% worked in clerical or sales jobs, 12% as proprietors, and 12% as professional or managerial.

Marital Status of Parents

The majority of residents came from homes in which both parents were present. However, there was significant family disruption in the history of these residents. About one-third of them reported parents separated or divorced or one or both parents were deceased.

Family Size and Birth Order of Residents

About 8% of the residents were "only children" and almost 60% had three or more siblings. Seventeen percent had one sibling, and 15% had two. About 30% of the residents were the first-born child in their family, 35% were the second born, 21% third, and 15% were the fourth or subsequent child.

Sexual Behavior

Incestuous relationships were reported by 30% of the female residents at *414,* while males disclaimed any such involvements. According to Wathey and Densen-Gerber (1976), incestuous relationships appear to be common among females who develop drug dependency. Results of a survey conducted by Odyssey House indicate that 35% of the residents had been involved in an incestuous relationship, 38% being female and 25% being male (MacLennan, 1975; Wathey and Densen-Gerber, 1976).

In summary, residents came from working-class homes with more disruption from divorce or death than usual. There was typically more than one child in the family. Incestuous relationships for the females exceeds what is thought to be customary, but was similar to that commonly reported among female members of therapeutic communities.

Perception of Parents

Parents of all residents of *414* were mailed a questionnaire that examined the temporal relationship between a variety of psychosocial problems and the onset of drug abuse. Fifty percent of the questionnaires were completed and returned. The results indicated that most parents (70%) felt that their children's problems predated the onset of the use of drugs. The remaining 30% indicated that their children started having problems coincident with or subsequent to first use of drugs. On the average, parents first noticed that their children were having problems around the age of 12. Involvement with drugs began, on the average, at age 16. A great majority (89%) of parents disapproved of some of their children's friends. Of these, fully 57% indicated that these friendships preceded rather than followed the onset of drug use. Parents in our study frequently reported having sought some sort of professional counseling for their children prior to the child's involvement with drugs (see Brook et al., 1976 for additional information).

Academic Program

Just over a third of the residents were enrolled in a 5-year college preparatory program when they last attended school, with 27% having been enrolled in technical programs and the rest in special education programs. The latter two programs prepare individuals for specific trades or skills. During this time, 51% of students in the London system, as a whole, were enrolled in the 5-year program (Portis & Powell, 1972).

Last Grade Completed and Number of Grades Repeated

The average grade completed for the residents of *414* was grade nine. Only a few of the residents had attended a university or college and a small proportion reported graduation from high school. Over 20% did not advance further than elementary school and 7% repeated one or more grades. Half (51%) reported average grades between 60 and 69 (C averages) during the final year of school; the distribution approximates a normal curve.

School Records and IQ

The Wechsler Adult Intelligence Scale (WAIS) was administered to a random sample of 30 residents. Academic records were obtained for 20 residents from the schools last attended (every sixth person every admitted into treatment). Fourteen of the residents who completed the intelligence test (WAIS) were also in this sample, which allowed the relationship between WAIS scores and school performance for these residents to be investigated.

Fully one-half of this subsample dropped out of school

before the end of the academic year. This figure is much higher than the 14.3% dropout rate for the London school population as a whole (Portis & Powell, 1972). Recorded comments by guidance counselors and other school officials stressed poor attendance and disciplinary problems. A frequent observation was that these students spent less than the minimum amount of time required on daily homework assignments and they tended not to be involved with extracurricular school activities.

Results of the WAIS test indicate that these drug users were normal in intellectual functioning (mean full-scale IQ was 108). This finding is consistent with reports of other studies dealing with drug-dependent youths (cf. Kramer, 1972; Smart & Jones, 1970). Thus, the drug users' poor academic performance was not due to intellectual impairment, but rather to a lack of participation in the educational process. It has been suggested that the use of drugs (Whitehead, 1971), especially a heavy use of drugs (Smart & Jones, 1970), is incompatible with regular school attendance and successful performance.

History of Drug Use

Age at First Use

A small proportion of residents report their first use of drugs before the age of 13 and 60% had their first experience with drugs by the time they were 16. The mean age for first use of illicit drugs is 16 years. The sequence of drug use was not always consistent, however; everyone used some type of "softer" drugs, alcohol, nicotine, or marihuana before using amphetamines. All the residents used drugs orally prior to intravenous use.

Duration of Regular Drug Use

Residents tended to have fairly long histories of drug use, with only a small proportion reporting regular use extending less than 6 months before admission to *414*. Twenty percent report using drugs regularly for 6 to 12 months, 15% for 1 to 2 years, 15% for 2 to 3 years, and 49% for over 3 years. The mean length of time reported for the regular use of drugs is more than 2 years. Such histories of drug use are, of course, far shorter than those displayed by heroin addicts in other therapeutic communities.

Drugs of Choice

The residents were polydrug users at admission with 100% of them using speed, marihuana, and alcohol on a regular basis. Forty-seven percent reported the occasional use of heroin.

The residents of *414* were typical amphetamine abusers, using high doses injected intravenously. The daily dosage depended on factors such as availability of the drug and the social setting in which the drug was taken. Kalant (1973) studied amphetamine users and reported a daily dosage ranging from 50 to 2600 milligrams. The average daily dosage for the *414* residents was estimated to be 1100 milligrams based on self-reports. The residents reported the typical pattern of going on runs for 3 to 5 days at a time, then crashing with the help of other drugs (e.g., Valium) usually obtained illegally.

Consequences of Drug Use: Legal and Clinical

Trouble with the law is frequently a consequence of illicit drug use. Three-quarters of the residents had been involved with the criminal justice system with 10% involved in drug-related offenses such as trafficking in drugs, and 22% involved in charges that included both drug-related and non-drug-related offenses. Most commonly, the residents were arrested for possession of stolen property.

Prior to admission to *414,* all of the residents had received some type of psychosocial counseling. Fifty-three percent made suicide attempts. Eighty-three percent sought treatment specifically for drug-related problems. In most cases, the treatment received was either crisis intervention at an emergency unit of a general hospital or short term on an outpatient basis. Several residents were hospitalized in psychiatric units of general hospitals or special wards for adolescents in psychiatric hospitals. Frequently they were uncooperative and unruly patients. None of the residents had been in a therapeutic community prior to *414.*

Psychological Characteristics

The Minnesota Multiphasic Personality Inventory (MMPI) was administered to residents at the time of admission. It provided a measure of the level of psychological disturbance manifested by these adolescents.

Overall Profiles

Four clinical scales and the *F* validity scale were in excess of *T*-score 80: Depression, Psychopathic Deviance, Psychasthenia, and Schizophrenia. The remaining scales were in excess of *T*-score 70. The composite profile for the residents described a population characterized by schizoid bizarreness, coupled with psychopathic features, and a sense of hopelessness (cf. Lachar, 1974; Marks et al., 1974). They were agitated, depressed, preoccupied with themselves, haunted by somatic complaints, and superficial in their interpersonal relationships. Logical thinking was constricted, ideas were strongly influenced by paranoid thoughts, and rational concentration on problems was severely impaired. The composite profile is suggestive of a population that is impulsive and given to acting out in bizarre ways. These personality traits are often associated with a poor prognosis for treatment (cf. Dahlstrom et al., 1975).

Patalano (1976) reports similar personality traits among younger residents of Odyssey House (see also Carlin, Detzer, & Strauss, 1978).

Summary of the Description of the Residents

The residents who were admitted to *414* tended to be relatively young and to come from working-class homes where about 40% of the marriages were disrupted. They were of normal intelligence as measured by the WAIS, but in terms of academic performance, they were underachievers. All the residents used amphetamines at some time and two-thirds indicated that it was their drug of choice when they entered treatment at *414*. They have well-established careers as drug users and were suffering some clinical, legal, and emotional problems in conjunction with their use of drugs.

Psychologically, residents were quite disturbed when they entered treatment. As a group, they displayed signs of a mixed personality type with psychopathic and schizoid features with depression.

The Comparison Group

The relative deviance of these patterns of behavior and psychological functioning can be determined by studying a sample of 24 local seconday school students who served as a normative comparison group. These students had no history of drug use, as was true of a majority of high school students in Canada in 1971 (cf. Smart & Whitehead, 1974). They were typical high school students from grades 10, 11 and 12. All were single and lived with their parents at the time of initial testing. About 20% were from broken homes, which is less than the *414* residents. None had received counseling or had records of suicide attempts or police involvement. Their average age was

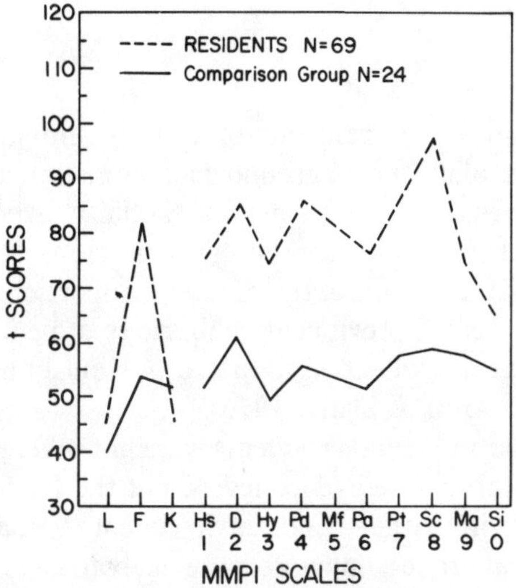

Fig. 4.1 Composite MMPL Profile for Residents of 414 and Comparison Group of High School Students

17 years and their mean grade in school (grade 11) was appropriate for their age.

The MMPI profiles of the high school students were found to be considerably less elevated than those of *414* residents (Figure 4.1). The several minor elevations that were found can be interpreted as reflecting normal rebelliousness among maturing adolescents. The profile comparison provides a good visual indication of the magnitude of psychological disturbance experienced by the *414* residents. Psychometrically the differences between these two groups are statistically significant on all scales.

Hence, in both behavioral and psychological terms, persons who entered treatment at *414* were experiencing considerable dysfunction. Their condition was serious, their difficulties were many, and their ability to cope was minimal. To some extent, it is out of this desperation that they made the decision to enter a therapeutic community that promised no prompt cure, but a supportive atmosphere where they might change.

SEX DIFFERENCES

Male and female residents of *414* are similar to one another in terms of most background characteristics, age, religion, family background, and residential mobility. About 85% of both males and females had received previous treatment for drug use, but a significantly greater proportion of females (93%) had received previous psychiatric treatment than males (55%). About half of each group had previously made suicide attempts (cf. Aron & Daily, 1976).

The male and female residents were not different from one another insofar as intelligence levels, but the females did perform better within the school environment. Females were as likely to repeat grades, but were more likely to have a B average in their school grades. Females were also more likely to be enrolled in special education programs whereas the males were more likely to be enrolled in technical programs.

Upon admission to *414*, male and female residents manifested some statistically significant differences on the MMPI. Females scored higher than the males on Scales *F,* (femininity); *Pd* (psychopathic deviate); *Pa* (paranoia); and *Sc* (schizophrenia). Males scored higher on Scale *L.* However, these statistical differences did not alter the basic schizoid and psychopathic features of the personality that characterized both males and females (Figure 4.2). Females appeared less depressed, more paranoid, and more withdrawn than their male counterparts.

It is possible, as Cooperstock (1971) suggests, that females are inhibited by cultural norms from acting out in deviant ways and are not as likely to get involved in drug abuse as are males. The small minority who do get involved may, in fact, be more deviant in terms of psychopathology than their male counterparts. De Leon (1974b), in his study of residents of Phoenix House, presented some evidence that supports this notion. Female residents of Phoenix House displayed significantly more pathology on a number of psychological measures than

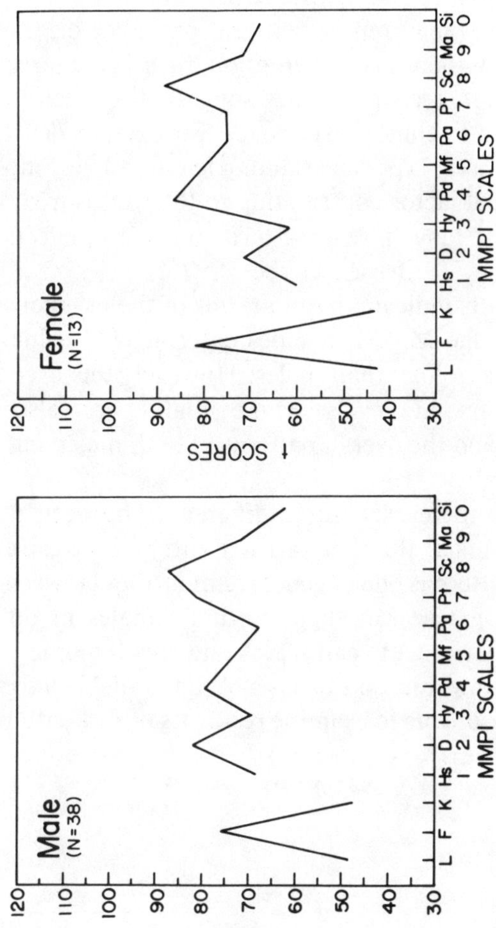

Fig. 4.2 Composite MMPL Profile for Males & Females at Time of Admission (1972)

males. De Leon concluded that addiction may relate to or express a more serious and complex psychological disturbance for women than for men. In contrast, Klinge, Vaziri, and Lennox (1976) suggest that some of the reported differences between the sexes may reflect bias and prejudice on the part of clinicians and their instrumentation rather than real differences. However, recent evidence suggests that such bias is inversely related to clinical experience (Stricker, 1977). The high incidence of incest experience among female adolescents may be a psychological factor contributing to their measured deviance because incest may have long-term traumatic effects on the victim (Wathey & Densen-Gerber, 1976).

The results indicate that, in terms of the psychopathology measured on the MMPI, females entering *414* exhibit somewhat more pathology than males. However, this excess in pathology occurs at levels where males are also clearly pathological and the overall patterns of both males and females are similar.

In brief, there exist some differences between male and female residents at the time of their entry into treatment, but the overall pattern is one of general similarities between the two sexes. Existing research suggests that females might be less amenable to treatment than males and this hypothesis will be considered. However, on the basis of the available information, it appears reasonable to examine residents of *414* without reference to their sex.

Chapter 5

RESULTS: THE WAY THEY ARE

This chapter first examines the behavioral and psychological functioning of former residents 10 months and 4 years after leaving *414* and then examines the impact of amount of treatment on the level of functioning at follow-up.

The number of days spent in residence at *414* is used as the index of the amount of treatment received by residents. It is a commonly held belief within therapeutic communities that the length of time spent in residence is positively related to behavioral improvement and that those who split quickly return to the street life of drug abuse. Attempts are made to assess the validity of this notion.

Behavioral Functioning

Marital Status and Children

On admission most residents were single although two who had been married were estranged from their partners.

Several residents had been cohabitating, but these tended to be temporary arrangements.

At the 10-month follow-up, the majority of former residents were still single. Two, who were both residents, subsequently married and two others were living common-law. At the 4-year follow-up, one-third of the former residents were married and living with their partner while an additional 14% were living common-law. Nine percent were separated or divorced. Of those who were married, most (65%) had one child, and a few (9%) had two or more children. None of those living in common-law arrangements had children with their current partners.

Residential Mobility

Former residents displayed fairly high rates of residential mobility. At the first follow-up, former residents had moved at least once in the 10 months since leaving the program, with a mean of three moves for the group. Four years later, only 24% had more than three residences in the previous year. Only a small proportion of residents (2%) lived with parents prior to entering treatment at *414.* The majority were either living alone or with drug-using friends. At the 10-month follow-up, 31% were living alone, 29% with their parents, 11% with drug-using friends, 22% with non-drug-using friends, and 7% with their spouse or common-law partners. At the 4-year follow-up, almost 14% were living alone, 5% were living with drug-using friends, 13% with non-drug-using friends, and 22% with their parents. Forty-five percent were living with their spouses or common-law partners.

Religion

At the 4-year follow-up, the proportion of those who identified themselves as Roman Catholic remained fairly constant, at about 30%. A large increase occurred in the "None" or "No preference" categories with the defections coming from the Protestant denominations.

The passage of time did not influence attendance at religious services. Very few of the former residents at the time of the 4-year follow-up were practicing members of a church. The majority attended services only irregularly. Roman Catholics tended to be more regular in their church attendance than Protestants, but Fundamental Protestants were the most active.

Employment—Education

On admission, former residents were unemployed dropouts from school. At the 4-year follow-up twice as many residents were working regularly than at the 10-month follow-up (82% and 44%, respectively), but of these only 35% worked all 12 months of the preceding year, the others worked an average of 7 months. Their employment record displayed more stability at the 4-year follow-up than at the 10-month follow-up.

Two-thirds had held the same job for the prior year compared to only 31% who did so previously. Only six former residents held the same job for more than 2 years prior to the 4-year follow-up.

Most (85%) residents who worked were employed in the capacity of skilled, semiskilled, or unskilled laborers. Three-quarters indicated they were satisfied with their current employment, one-half intended to remain in their current line of work, and one-half aspired to higher status jobs in the future. Few residents were engaged in supplementary training to improve current skills. While many graduates of therapeutic communities continue to work within therapeutic communities, none of the former *414* residents were working within a therapeutic community, nor in other types of social service positions.

At the 10-month follow-up, one-quarter of the former residents were attending school, whereas by the 4-year follow-up, it had declined to one-fifth. The average grade level increased from grade 9 to grade 10. Those who resumed their formal education after leaving *414* did better in school than they had previously. Most were enrolled in specific training programs at the community college level. Three former residents were attending university.

Many of the former residents had street debts, usually for dope, when they initiated treatment at *414.* More than 70% were in debt at the time of the 4-year follow-up, and 42% had debts in excess of $1000. However, the source of the debt had changed. The most common debts accumulated were for car loans, house mortgages, credit card purchases, and legal fees. Just under three-quarters had some savings in the bank or in government bonds.

Use of Drugs

When admitted to *414,* residents were heavily involved with illicit drugs, with a preference for amphetamines. Ten months after treatment, 53% reported the occasional use of alcohol, and 80% reported the same 4 years later. While the amount of absolute alcohol or the number of drinks consumed per drinking occasion is not known, it is known that alcoholic beverages tended to be consumed at least every other day. Some reported solitary drinking, but most used alcoholic beverages in social settings and in bars with friends. The majority of former residents do not perceive their current use of alcohol as a problem, but three former residents sought professional assistance for alcohol abuse.

At the 10-month follow-up, 34% occasionally used marihuana. The proportion of users increased to 51% at the 4-year follow-up, 20% using it 11 or more times per month. The use of speed declined considerably since 1972. Eighty-nine percent at the 10-month follow-up and 93% at the 4-year follow-up reported no use of amphetamines. Those who reported using it did so fewer than five times. None who used speed at the 10-month follow-up reported doing so in 1976.

At the 10-month follow-up, three residents were current users of heroin. In the month prior to the 4-year follow-up 51 persons (93%) reported *no* use of heroin. Three used heroin fewer than 5 times, and one more than 10 times.

Former residents gave reasons for no longer being involved with illicit drugs. Fifty-five percent said that drug involvement would be unproductive in their current life-style. Eighteen percent said they no longer needed drugs to offset psychological and emotional deficits and that the real struggle was not in shifting away from drugs but in recognizing and actualizing their potential. Eleven percent were deterred from continuing drug abuse for fear of physiological damage. Another reason frequently given was that current friends would be offended. This was evidenced in the initial resistance that we received from some residents about completing the follow-up questionnaire. They feared that their past would be revealed to their spouse or close friend.

Record of Arrest

At the 10-month follow-up the proportion of arrests was 25% and at the 4-year follow-up it was 27%, compared to 78% prior to admission to *414*. The proportion of the former residents arrested remained about the same, but the proportion who spent time in jail increased. Eighty-six percent of those arrested in 1976 actually spent time in jail, whereas in 1973 64% of those arrested spent time in jail. One-third of those arrested in 1976 had also been arrested in 1973.

Self-Injury

The incidence of suicide attempts and other forms of self-injurious behaviors changed significantly between the time of admission (53%) and the year prior to the 4-year follow-up (6%)

Three persons still involved with drugs had sought additional psychological assistance and two of three were incarcerated at the time of their self-injury.[1]

Relationship with Parents

Eighty-two percent of residents on admission characterized their relationship with their parents as poor, and 18% as good. At the 4-year follow-up, 93% reported this relationship to be excellent or good, 7% said that their relationship continues to be poor, and these residents were either incarcerated or abusing drugs.

Psychological Functioning

When the adolescent amphetamine abusers entered *414,* they manifested severe psychological disturbances (Figure 5.1). The composite MMPI profile displays marked elevations on four of the clinical scales: Schizophrenia (Scale 8), Psychoasthenia (Scale 7), Psychopathic Deviate (Scale 4), and Depression (Scale 2). All are in excess of three standard deviations above the mean for normals. At the 10-month follow-up, the personality pattern still borders on abnormality, but the serverity in psychopathology is significantly reduced on all clinical scales except Hypomania.

The configuration of the composite profile at this time suggested poor impulse control, superficial interpersonal relationships, immaturity, self-centered or egocentric thought processes, but a marked decline in depression. The group no longer reflected the same sense of hopelessness evident at the initial testing.

Psychological functioning was further improved at the the 4-year follow-up. No clinical scales were in excess of *T*-score

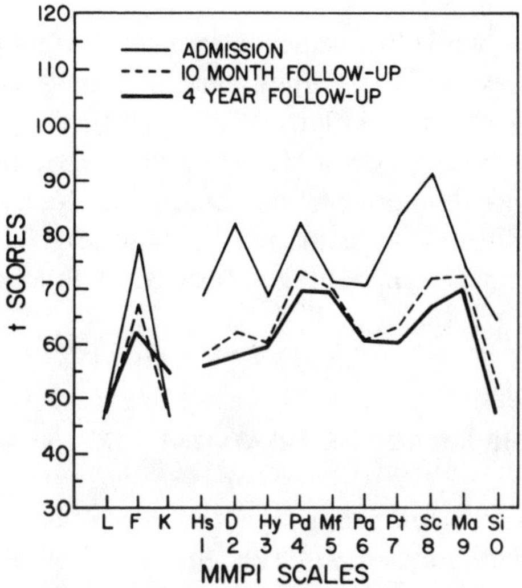

Fig. 5.1 Composite MMPL Profile for Three Time Periods: Admission, 10 month Follow-up and 4 Year Follow-up

70, conventionally interpreted as the border of normality and abnormality. The composite MMPI profile manifested less psychological disturbance and agitation, increased sense of self-worth and personal satisfaction, fewer and less pronounced mood swings, increased concentration and rational thinking, decreased bizarre and unusual perceptions, greater sociability, and less despair than characterized their earlier functioning.

The results of the two follow-up studies indicated a marked improvement of former residents over their condition when they entered *414.* Antisocial patterns of behavior, characterized by the abuse of drugs, unemployment, and difficulty with the police, had been altered. Psychological functioning was considerably improved between the two follow-up periods, with former residents displaying increased psychological stability. By 1976, about 4 years after leaving treatment, the extreme and competing factors of depression, agitation, and overall dysfunction subsided.

However, while the residents were less deviant psychologically and behaviorally than they were on admission, they were by no means normal in that as a group they still displayed elevated profiles. Considerable improvement should not be mistaken for an idyllic notion of complete cure. Nevertheless, the provocative question remains whether the level of behavioral and psychological functioning measured at follow-up can be attributed to treatment at *414*.

Assessing the Impact of Treatment

Three major competing hypotheses may account for the improved functioning of *414* residents at follow-up: first, improvement may be associated with background characteristics or resources that residents brought with them to *414;* second, improved functioning may be a product of treatment received by residents *after* leaving *414;* third, improved functioning may be associated with amount of treatment received at *414*.

Impact of Background

It is theoretically possible that the background characteristics of the residents was a determinant in the later development of favorable levels of psychological and behavioral functioning. Some investigators systematically classify patients in terms of background or demographic constructs (see, for example, Sells & Simpson, 1976), to successfully match patients to treatment. The underlying assumption is that patient background may significantly interact with, or predict, later improvement.

In this study a one-way analysis of covariance was used in order to examine the relationship between background variables and measures of outcome at follow-up, employing time in treatment as the covariate.

Results showed that most background variables measured on admission to *414* such as socioeconomic status of the family,

family stability, family size, the resident's age and sex, the age at first drug use, duration of drug use, and the level of education[2] were not significantly related to behavioral success at either of the follow-up periods. Some relationships are manifest at one follow-up period but not the other. These relationships are difficult to interpret and may not be meaningful since they do not persist across time and are least likely to appear at the 4-year follow-up.

In order to complete this analysis, psychological functioning on admission was treated as a background variable to assess whether this had an impact on performance at follow-up. In examining these hypotheses, psychological functioning was measured in terms of the MMPI scales and behavioral functioning was measured in terms of the summary measure provided by an adaptation of the Chambers and Inciardi (1974) criteria. The criteria were use of drugs, involvement with the criminal justice system, and employment or education. The Chambers and Inciardi Index characterized former residents as "successful" if they met all three criteria; "partially successful" if they met two of the three; and "failures" if they met one or none of the criteria.[3]

In order to statistically control for time in treatment an analysis of covariance, with time in treatment as the covariate, was calculated. The results indicated that no MMPI scale at the time of admission was a significant factor in later success or failure of the residents at the follow-up periods.

Impact of Supplementary Treatment

Subsequent to leaving *414,* and prior to the 10-month follow-up, 23% of the former residents sought some type of supplementary treatment, most commonly from clinics or hospitals, although a few participated in long-term residential programs. During the 12 months prior to the 4-year follow-up, 29% received additional psychological assistance. A minority participated in residential programs for drug abuse while others spent a short time at a psychiatric hospital. These events were usually precipitated by a personal crisis or a psychiatric evaluation ordered by a court. The others sought counseling on an outpatient basis from professional sources such as physicians. This was commonly short-term therapy involving one or two visits and a prescription of mild tranquilizers. The presenting problems were usually depression associated with situational reactions, for example, marriage, a break-up with a girlfriend or boyfriend, or disillusionment about being unemployed.

Results of analysis showed that at neither follow-up period was the receipt of supplementary treatment significantly associated with either behavioral or psychological functioning.

Impact of Treatment at 414

If treatment at *414* was effective, a positive relationship between exposure to treatment at *414* and level of functioning at the time of follow-up would be expected. Exposure to treatment is measured in terms of the number of days spent in treatment. At the 10-month follow-up, the length of time spent in treatment was positively correlated with behavioral functioning as measured by the Chambers and Inciardi Index ($r = .40$; $p < .01$). Time in treatment accounts for 20% of the variance in behavioral functioning and is significantly correlated with some measures of psychological functioning at the time of the 10-month follow-up. The longer the residents had been in treatment, the less likely they were to be depressed, the more positive was their self-concept, and the more sociable and extroverted they were. Similar results did not obtain at the time of the 4-year follow-up when there was no significant relationship between time spent in treatment and behavioral functioing or psychological adjustment.

Thus, the rather considerable improvement manifested by former residents at the time of follow-up, especially 4 years after leaving treatment, was not a function of the amount of treatment to which they were exposed while at *414*.

These mixed results may mean that the conditon of the residents when they entered treatment influenced how long they would stay in treatment. To assess this, days in treatment was correlated with the background variables and scores on MMPI scales obtained on admission. Only 1 of the 24 background variables was significant. Residents coming from homes disrupted by divorce, separation, or death were more likely to spend less time in treatment ($r = .26$, $p < .05$) than those persons whose homes were not disrupted.

There is little relationship between the psychological condition of the residents on admission and the amount of time spent in treatment. Depression and social extroversion were the only two psychological scales significantly correlated with the length of time spent in treatment. Residents who were more socially oriented and less depressed stayed in treatment longer than those residents who were depressed and introverted. The finding concerning depression is closely paralleled in other studies (e.g., McFarlain, Cohen, Yoder, & Guidry, 1977). The strength of the relationship is fairly weak and does not occur on scales that principally characterize the psychopathology of residents on admission.

Sex Differences

Key background variables such as employment status, drug abuse histories, or arrest records do not differentiate males from females at admission to *414* but some evidence suggests that females display slightly more psychopathology. However, sex differences in psychological functioning are not evident at the 10-month or 4-year follow-up (Figure 5.2).

At the first follow-up, a greater proportion of males were failures according to the Chambers and Inciardi Index than females (36.6% versus 28.6%, respectively). At the second follow-up, 22% of the males and 14% of the females were failures. However, these differences are not statistically significant. At

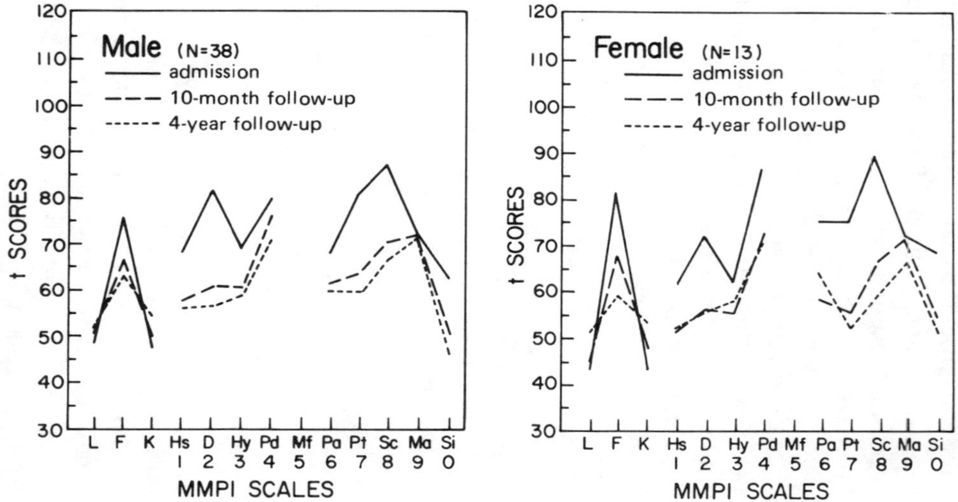

Fig. 5.2 Composite MMPL Profile for Three Different Time Periods: Admission, 10 Months Follow-up and Four Year Follow-up

the 10-month follow-up, time spent in treatment was significantly correlated with behavioral functioning among former residents ($r = .40$; $p < .01$), but this correlation was completely a function of males ($r = .52$; $p < .01$) and not of females ($r =$ .09; NS). However, among males there was no significant relationship between behavioral functioning at the 10-month follow-up and at the 4-year follow-up, whereas among females this relationship was a strong one ($r = .62$; $p < .05$).

Males and females display most of the improvements in psychological functioning at the time of the 10-month follow-up, with additional improvement by the 4-year follow-up. Between follow-ups males became less depressed, more socially extroverted, and more satisfied with themselves. Females maintained the improvements between intake and first follow-up and their scores indicated that they were satisfied with themselves.

There is little association between psychological functioning at admission and how long either males or females stayed in treatment. There is little relationship between how long males or females stayed in treatment and later psychological functioning, as measured by the MMPI. Specifically, at admission, none of the scores on clinical scales are associated with length of time spent in treatment among females. Among males only the Social Introversion/Extroversion Scale has such a relationship and it is small. At the time of the 10-month follow-up, time in treatment is not significantly correlated with scores of females on any of the clinical scales and at the time of the 4-year follow-up only Hypochondriasis has such a relationship. Among males, time in treatment is associated with scores on three scales (Depression, Hypomania, and Social Introversion/ Extroversion) of the MMPI at the time of the 10-month follow-up, but all of these disappear by the time of the 4-year follow-up.

Thus, we find no marked differences between males and females when both follow-up times are taken into consideration. Time in treatment is associated with behavioral functioning among males at the time of the 10-month follow-up, but the relationship is nonexistent at the 4-year follow-up among both males and females. There is no particular pattern of differences between males and females in terms of the relationship between time in treatment and psychological functioning. The dominant pattern is one of similarities involving a lack of statistically significant differences. Therefore, we find little evidence that males and females bring different strengths or weaknesses to treatment or that they respond differently to it.

Summary

This chapter examined what happened to former residents of *414* both 10 months and 4 years after having left treatment. Former residents displayed considerable improvement in behavioral and psychological terms. This held true for both male and female residents.

The amount of time residents spent in treatment was generally not related to background variables of the residents or to their behavioral and psychological functioning when they entered treatment. There was little evidence that length of exposure to treatment was significantly related to behavioral or psychological outcome when measured at both follow-up periods. The receipt of supplementary treatment after *414* did not account for outcome at follow-up.

Chapter 6

DISCUSSION, EVALUATION, AND IMPLICATIONS

414 was established in order to meet a perceived need for treatment of young amphetamine abusers. An additional objective of the *414* project was to evaluate its efficacy and add to what was, and remains today, a quite sparse literature on the effectiveness of therapeutic communities in the management of addictions.

The community was established and existed for 2½ years. During this time, 156 young people were treated for periods ranging from a few hours to a 1½ years. The major component of the evaluation was a series of two follow-up studies of a sample of 55 former residents conducted 10 months and 4 years after treatment. These 55 are not a random sample of former residents, but they are highly representative of all residents of *414*. The purpose of the study was to report the experience of this therapeutic community and to examine the extent to which exposure to treatment at *414* accounted for variation in measures of outcome assessed at two follow-up periods.

The Residents

At the time they entered treatment at *414,* the residents were experiencing severe behavioral and psychological difficulties. They were heavily involved in the drug culture and experienced dysfunctions in various areas of their life that in most cases preceded drug abuse, as well as other problems stemming from their use of drugs. The resulting constellation of psychological disturbance and deviant behavior was defined as problematic by their families, the community, and themselves.

The most appropriate psychological diagnosis for the residents when they entered treatment was personality disturbance. Specifically the residents manifested the psychopathological signs of both an antisocial personality and latent schizophrenia. This unusual combination of personality traits interacted to keep the adolescents in a state of flux. It was this pattern that led us to characterize them as immature (cf. Brook et al., 1976). The psychopathic features modify the schizophrenic facets and mitigate against psychosis and a true schizophrenic disturbance. At the same time, the schizoid features function in ways that reduce the likelihood of the development of a true sociopathic personality.

The adolescent amphetamine users may share personality features with both of these diagnostic categories, but in fact belong to neither. Instead, they are too superficial, impoverished, eccentric, and bizarre to be good sociopaths; yet they retain sufficient ego control to ward off a schizophrenic disorder. A similar pattern has been observed by Ellinwood (1967, 1969) and we agree with him that the adolescent amphetamine abuser is best characterized as manifesting a pseudo-psychopathic schizophrenic disturbance (cf. Freedman, Kaplan, & Sadock, 1972).

Kalant (1973) reports that one of the most frequently observed effects of chronic amphetamine use is a drug-induced psychotic reaction that is often misdiagnosed as schizophrenia. She argues that the condition tends to be transitory and usually dissipates with the withdrawl of the drug but that "in a small but appreciable number of cases, the persistence of symptoms for a long time after drug withdrawal indicates that amphetamine may act as a precipitating factor in the onset of true schizophrenia."

There was no evidence that amphetamine abuse among *414* residents precipitated the onset of true schizophrenia. None of the residents at follow-up were maintained on phenothiazines for schizophrenic-type reactions and only one of the 55 residents was hospitalized at the 10-month follow-up and he was not diagnosed as schizophrenic.

Chronic use of intravenously administered amphetamines has been reported to progress to heroin addiction in that heroin is a good drug to use while coming off a run or while crashing (Le Dain, 1973). Malcolm (1973a) cites the report of the Le Dain Commission as strong evidence of progression from amphetamines to heroin.

Information on the status of 55 residents who were followed up challenges this view in that while some residents used heroin, none were heroin addicts, and only one female used heroin regularly.

The Results of the Follow-up Studies

The principal results are summarized as follows. First, in both behavioral and psychological terms, former residents displayed considerable improvement at both follow-up periods over their condition when they entered treatment. Second, there is some evidence 10 months after termination of treatment that behavioral functioning at follow-up was positively associated with the amount of time spent in treatment. This relationship did not prevail 4 years after termination of treatment. Third, functioning at the time of follow-up was not a product of background characteristics, behavioral or psychological condition at the time of admission, or supplementary treatment received after leaving *414.* Fourth, in spite of the improvement shown by residents in behavioral and psychological terms, former residents still displayed elevated psychological profiles indicative of some degree of disturbance; the same is also reflected in their behavior as they continued to manifest fairly high rates of deviance. Fifth, when only one follow-up period is considered it appears that males and females displayed a differential response to treatment, but when both follow-up periods are considered there is insufficient evidence to warrant an inference of differential response to treatment.

How Well is Well?

In order to obtain an additional perspective on the functioning of former residents, the data were subjected to ideographic analysis. Two clinical psychologists registered by the Board of Psychologists in the Province of Ontario served as independent raters. Both had at least 5 years postdoctoral experience, one was chief of psychological services at a university teaching hospital and the other was coordinator of the clinical program within a university department of psychology. Both were skilled in diagnostic and prognostic interpretations of the MMPI and tended to be identified with the behavioral orientation in psychology. Neither psychologist had previous contact with the residents or the treatment program at *414.* The two psychologists did the ratings independently and were paid a fee for each clinical assessment. All instructions were provided in writing.

The assessments were conducted in two stages. In the first stage, information provided to the raters came from data collected at the 4-year follow-up; in the second stage, information came from data collected on admission and at the 10-month follow-up. Summary descriptions of behavioral and psychological information were provided, one case at a time, and the psychologists were asked to rate each person's adjustment as excellent, above average, average, or below average.[1] They were

Table 6.1 Ratings by Clinical Psychologists of 414 Residents on the Basis of Idiographic Data

	Rater 1		*Rater 2*			
	No.	*Percent*	*No.*	*Percent*	*Average Percent*	r[a]
Current adjustment						
Excellent	5	9.8	2	3.9	7	
Above average	10	19.6	4	7.8	14	
Average	15	29.4	15	29.4	29	
Below average	20	39.1	30	58.8	49	
Unable to form opinion	1	2.0			1	0.79
Current need for psychological assistance						
Definitely	16	31.4	17	33.3	31	
Likely	14	27.5	14	27.5	28	
Unnecessary	21	41.2	20	39.2	41	0.79
Degree of change						
Definitely improved	29	56.9	18	35.3	47	
Somewhat improved	12	23.5	17	33.3	29	
About the same	1	1.9	12	23.5	13	
Some deterioration	8	15.7	4	7.8	12	0.52

[a]r = Interrater reliability.

also asked to respond to the question: Does the person need psychological assistance? with answers of definitely, likely, unnecessary.

On both of these items interrater reliability (Winer, 1971) was reasonably high at r=.71 (Table 6.1). The psychologists rated the current level of adjustment of 7% of the former residents to be excellent, 14% above average, 29% average, and 49% below average. Psychological assistance was judged to be unnecessary in 41% of the cases, likely necessary in 28% of the cases, and definitely necessary for the other 31% of the former residents. Thus, half the former residents were rated below average in functioning and 60% were seen as likely to be in need of further psychological assistance.

The State of the Art

The finding that length of exposure to treatment at *414* has no demonstrable impact on later functioning of residents violates two sets of expectations. First, at the beginning, we expected that the therapeutic community was apt to meet the needs of adolescent amphetamine abusers (see, for example, Brook & Whitehead, 1973a; Brook, Kaplun, & Whitehead 1974).

Second, it violates the expectations that stem from favorable reports and commentaries on other therapeutic communities. There are no sound follow-up studies that clearly demonstrate that treatment in therapeutic communities leads to improvement that would otherwise not have occurred. However, we continue to receive the sense that treatment of addictions is efficacious (see, for example, Pin, Martin, & Walsly, 1976; O'Brien, 1976; Charuvastra & Charbeneaux, 1977; Kaufman & De Leon, 1978); and this is even true in some of the better contemporary research. For example, a major study of the behavior of drug abusers after they leave a variety of treatment programs has been conducted by the National Institute on Drug Abuse (NIDA). The Drug Abuse Reporting Programs (DARP) includes follow-up interviews conducted an average of 4 years after addicts left treatment. Therapeutic communities are one of the five types of treatment programs that were analyzed. Sells, Simpson, Joe, Demaree, Savage, and Lloyd (1976) cautiously report their results and say that "genuine post treatment effects were found," and indicate that "TC patients compare very favourably with those from Methadone Maintenance and in some cases look superior." Ginzburg (1976) calls it a "landmark study" and indicates that its results challenge some long-held assumptions about treatment. When former clients are found not to be using drugs at follow-up the implication is that this is a result of treatment. Even receiving supplementary treatment is taken to be a product of successful treatment:

> At the time of follow-up nearly 30 percent were in treatment. This suggests that drug treatment "failures" are often not failures at all; rather, each treatment episode allows the drug abuser another opportunity to terminate illicit drug usage (Ginzburg, 1976).

The beneficial effects of treatment are said to be there whether one recognizes them or not:

> It appears that drug abusers change their life-styles gradually over time, and the traditional programs facilitate this gradual change. In many cases the changes are rapid and the results immediately evident; in others, the changes are slow and are *only perceived by the patient and the community* after *several* treatment experiences and *several* years. In a *minority* of cases there is no change at all (emphasis ours; Ginzburg, 1976).

Some appropriate caveats are included along the line that not all the credit for improvement can be given to treatment.

In this report, as in a later one (Sells, 1977), it is *implied,* not *stated,* that some change is related to treatment, but neither experimental nor correlational evidence is presented in support. We also found that our residents display high rates of improvement at follow-up, but their level of functioning bears little relationship to the amount of treatment while in residence or to supplementary treatment after they left.

Methodological Considerations

There are, as we have indicated, aspects of the design of the current evaluation that we wish were experimental (see, for example, Schriven, 1967). However, our procedures are consistent with many of the principles and practices in program evaluation suggested by Anderson and Ball (1978). Had we discovered an apparent effect of treatment it would have been useful to test some alternative hypotheses that might account for them. Since our findings are generally those of no apparent effect, we are not plagued by not being able to do some of the tests that we would have preferred to incorporate into the design.

Our experience leads us to make two additional methodological comments that have implications for future research. First, conclusions from long-term follow-up may differ considerably from those made on the basis of a short-term follow-up. At 10 months after having left treatment there is far more—although still limited—evidence that treatment may have had an independent effect on functioning than one would infer from the results of the 4-year follow-up. As Barr (1977) points out, if the strength of the Therapeutic Community (TC) is "its ability to alter the entire course of a person's life, its effectiveness can be validated only by following TC graduates over a period of years."

Second, multiple follow-up periods appear to be of considerable advantage in assisting researchers to sift out which factors are truly relevant to the impact of treatment. When many tests of statistical significance are conducted, some "significant" relationships will appear as a matter of chance. However, with multiple periods of follow-up one gets additional opportunities to discover these by examining whether they persist over time. We encourage other researchers to consider the possibility of incorporating such features into their designs.

Unexplained Variance

There are three other sets of factors that may account for the as yet unexplained variance: *history, regression,* and *maturation* (cf. Campbell & Stanley, 1963).

History

The first set, history, has to do with the diversity of experiences that former residents had during the months and years after leaving treatment. Depending on the efficacy of treatment and how long they stayed in treatment, some residents *may* have been better prepared to deal with life outside the therapeutic community than others. However, due to their youth, previous history of problems, level of psychological disturbance, and propensity for deviant behavior, residents may have had limited capacity to control their environment and to utilize their (possibly) enhanced skills for coping with life.

Other factors, such as how residents were received by their families or the ease they experienced in returning to school or getting a job, may have depended far more on factors beyond their control than how effectively they exercised their new skills in coping. In this sense, persons who stayed in treatment only a fairly short time may have had a share of positive experiences similar to those who stayed a much longer time.

Regression

The second set of factors that may account for some of the unexplained variance is regression. An effect of regression involves the unlikelihood of extreme or unusual performance being repeated on a successive trail. Statistically the repeat performance would be expected to be closer to the usual or average.

The decision of young people to enter *414* was momentous. They were asked to make a commitment to forego the use of drugs, to obey the rules of the house, and to stay in residence for at least 1 year. On the basis of our early clinical impressions and in terms of our current thinking, it is likely that residents entered treatment at a time of extreme psychological stress and disturbed behavior patterns. They may have entered treatment at their worst or close to it. If this was the case, then their behavior patterns shortly before entering treatment and their level of psychological dysfunction at the time of testing were observed when they were close to their peaks. Given such a situation, it would mean that in observing them at another time,

3, 6, or 12 months later, we would likely find, on the average, a lower level of dysfunction and deviance. Such a decrease would not have been caused by treatment, but would be an artifact of regression.

Maturation

The third set of factors that may well have operated is *maturation.* Maturation refers to processes that operate as a result of the passage of time rather than as a result of particular events. Factors involved in maturation can include such things as growing more tired, but the important one in this case was probably growing older.

The people who entered *414* did so at a fairly young age and they began using drugs and having problems at even younger ages. Many young people experience problems of adjustment during this period though they are not as serious as those of our residents. Nevertheless, in time they grow up, they learn to cope, they learn to adjust to society, and society learns to adapt to the new styles of the youth culture. The young people do not become just like the older ones, but there is accommodation that takes place and the world goes on.

Experimentation with the use of drugs has prevailed in many communities, but regular or frequent users have consistently been a small proportion of all users. In time, people get better, some of course get worse, but there are many forces operating in society that have the effect of guiding, pushing, encouraging, rewarding, punishing, shoving, and channeling persons into doing what society deems to be *right.* Having these experiences over an extended period of time may be the single most important variable in whether one improves. The opportunity to grow older may be the critical factor affecting treatment and the best treatment appears to be highly correlated with time. Time provides an opportunity not only to grow *older,* but also to *grow up,* to mature, and to leave irresponsibilities of youth behind (cf. Stang, 1977).

Many patterns of behavior displayed by former residents years after leaving treatment appear to be prosocial: they have married, taken jobs, and borrowed money to buy an automobile. These are the sorts of things that people can more likely do at age 23 than age 19.

We cannot test these hypotheses about history, regression, or maturation within the context of the present study. We can only speculate about them as we have been doing. But these speculations have implications for further research. We sense that the effects of history, regression, and maturation are not equally likely to be manifest at both follow-up periods. The effect of regression is apt to be greatest shortly after treatment has begun. In our study it would have confounded measurement at the time of the 10-month follow-up. Maturation would take longer to have its effect and was probably most prominent at the 4-year follow-up. The effect of history may well have been more variable over time, but we would not be surprised to find that it was manifest at the 10-month follow-up.

Rates of Retention

One of the typical measures of the efficacy of therapeutic communities is the success such programs have in retaining residents. This is usually expressed in terms of its reciprocal, that is, its rates of splitting. Split rates, as they are customarily called, are notoriously high. Some reports indicate that 90 to 95% of residents in therapeutic communities prematurely terminate treatment (cf. Brecher et al., 1972). More recently Glaser (1974b) has suggested that split rates are more on the order of 60 to 80%.

It is possible that split rates vary between programs depending on such things as characteristics of the program, characteristics of the residents, and whether residents enter the therapeutic community voluntarily or because of a court order that has jail as an alternative. Split rates are also affected by the definitions and procedures used in the calculations. Some programs calculate their split rate on the basis of only including persons who have been officially admitted, which in some cases involve as long as 6 to 9 months of probation. Others, on the other hand, calculate their split rates by including everyone who spends a night at the facility. The latter would, of course, produce higher rates of splitting than the former.

Glaser (1974b) differentiates between gross split rates and net split rates. Gross rates count every instance of splitting, including repeated splits by the same individual, while net rates take each person into account only once, allowing only one split per individual who is admitted. For *414,* the gross rate is 89% and the net rate is 83%.

Therapeutic communities have been criticized for their high split rates. For those working in the programs, the experience is often discouraging. At *414* we initiated various adjustments to the program so as to reduce the split rate. For example, we increased the number and variety of group experiences for residents. We made short-term modifications in the program such as increasing the rate of movement through the probationary and resident levels and including probationary residents in house camping trips and weekend activities. The effects of these adjustments were not studied experimentally. However, the observations on the part of the staff and some comparisons of the split rates during the different procedures suggest that they did not influence the rate of splitting.

The greatest effect these changes in program may have had was in improving the morale of residents and staff. Working intensively for long days with residents who then split is discouraging and contributes to "staff burn out," a phenomenon experienced at *414* (Brook & Whitehead, 1973a) and reported to exist at many other communities (see, for example, Freudenberger, 1976; Maslach, 1976). The adjustments to the program reduced the frustrations, disappointments, and "burn-out." Staff members were actively engaged in trying alternatives that provided hope that the rate of splitting would be reduced.

It has been suggested by Glaser (1974b) that split rates could be improved if therapeutic communities allowed methadone or other regimes of chemotherapy (see, for example, Hubbard, Judd, & Avery, 1978), but usually the "purists" within the therapeutic community movement oppose such suggestions. One hypothesis is that therapeutic communities tolerate these high rates out of a need to be exclusive. It can be argued that high split rates are functional in that they allow those who stay to believe that they are an elite group. This may lead to an enhancement of the self-concept among those who stay, but we have no data on this.

On the basis of our findings of the small amount of variance in measures of outcome accounted for by the amount of time spent in treatment, we believe that therapeutic communities ought not to worry too much about having low rates of retention. It may be that the major value of the therapeutic community is that it serves as a port in a behavioral or psychological storm, providing shelter during times of crisis. It is quite possible, however, that less expensive ways could be found to meet this objective.

Cost

No single figure best portrays the costs of operating the *414* program. There are a variety of criteria in terms of which monetary costs can be evaluated and each provides a different picture. Costs calculated on a per diem basis per resident are widely accepted as providing comparison across different types of facilities having similar goals.

During its history the total operating cost of *414* was $262,617. This includes renovations to the facility, but excludes the purchase price of the facility ($110,000), which is recoverable at a profit. The figure also excludes about $75,000, which is associated solely with research and not the delivery of treatment. The following analyses are based on the operating cost of $262,617.

The 156 residents admitted to *414* spent a total of 13,077 days in treatment. Thus, each day in treatment costs $20. For Daytop Village, the cost is $21; for Phoenix House, $10; and for Odyssey House, $19 (System Sciences, Inc., 1973a;b;c).

The per diem cost at *414* also compares favorably with that of a special unit for adolescent drug abusers at a local psychiatric hospital, $80 per day per patient. It compares even more favorably with a psychiatric unit in a general hospital that treated drug abusers at a cost of over $100 per day.

Unfortunately, we do not have information on the *efficacy* of these other programs that would allow us to precisely assess their relative *efficiency.* However, on the basis of the information we do have, it is clear that these other programs would need a level of effectiveness that would be four to five times as great as *414* in order to be equally efficient.

The following analysis must be viewed in a very guarded fashion. It is conducted in an attempt to provide estimates of the costs associated with producing certain outcomes. The outcomes are defined in two ways: (1) the Chambers and Inciardi criteria and (2) the assessments made by two clinical psychologists. All measures are based on the follow-up 4 years after residents left treatment and the results have been extrapolated to all 156 persons who ever received treatment at *414.*

Our version of the Chambers and Inciardi (1974) behavioral criteria, at the 4-year follow-up, indicated that 53% of the former residents were "totally successful," 27% "partially successful," and 20% "failures." Extrapolating these rates over all 156 persons treated at *414* and apportioning the costs of the program across these categories produces the following estimates. It costs, on the average, $3,164 for each completely successful resident or $2,100 for each resident that was either partially or completely successful.

When clinical judgments of success are used the estimates of costs are somewhat different. The clinicians, on the average, rated 50% of the former residents to be average, above average, or excellent in their level of functioning at follow-up. On the average, and extrapolated over all persons ever treated, these outcomes cost $1,683 per resident who is at least average at follow-up.

Therefore, in terms of the way we have calculated the costs, the estimates produced on the basis of behavioral functioning alone, using the Chambers and Inciardi criteria, are not greatly different (about 20 to 25%) from estimates that define favorable performance (at least average) on the basis of ratings by clinicians where both behavioral and psychological data are available.

The fact that we are unable to demonstrate a relationship between length of exposure to treatment and later functioning means that we cannot infer that any of these costs were *needed* in order to transform adolescent amphetamine abusers into somewhat more average persons.

Summary

When the "speed freaks" came on the scene they caused great consternation to people in the field of treatment as well as other sectors of the community. They were viewed as having a very poor prognosis and as being untreatable. The popular and professional wisdom was that they were crazy and they would become crazier in the future.

The experience of *414* in dealing with these young people offers a basis for revising such judgments. Adolescent amphetamine abusers did seek treatment; many stayed in treatment only a short time, but several stayed for a long time. When followed up they show considerable improvement although generally they are not what would conventionally be called normal. Their level of functioning at follow-up is not a function of the amount of exposure to treatment that they received at *414*. We have not been able to compare the residents to similar persons who never received treatment at *414*, but our analysis does include many residents who spent only hours or a few days at *414*. Unless there was something immensely therapeutic about crossing the threshold at 414 Dufferin Avenue they are about as close to a "no treatment" as we can get.

The fact that we are unable to directly account for the improvement displayed by residents is somewhat frustrating, but less important than the fact that we are able to test some theoretically and programmatically meaningful hypotheses. Funtioning at follow-up is not accounted for by time spent in treatment, treatment received after leaving *414,* the background characteristics of the residents when they entered treatment, or the behavioral or psychological functioning at the time residents entered treatment. We cannot know for sure what would have happened to them had *414* not existed. The literature on therapeutic communities is full of examples and comments (Frankel, Brook, & Whitehead, 1977) on the high rates of relapse among people who split. Fryholm, Gunne, and Huitfeldt (1976) provide similar evidence relative to amphetamine abusers. However, based on the results of the *414* experience, it appears that this may not be the case. It appears unlikely that in the absence of *414* they would have committed suicide or gone crazy; more likely they would have spent more time on the street and would have sought assistance from other facilities, possibly at a higher cost per day, but maybe for fewer days.

At the time of follow-up we asked the residents if they felt that they had been helped by their experiences at *414*: 3% indicated that they did not know; 26% said that they had been helped somewhat; and 71% said that they had definitely been helped.

The cost of delivering this help appears markedly lower than that for a general or psychiatric hospital, and, in this sense, *414* may have been reasonably efficient. It may be that there are still less costly ways of producing the same effect and having more efficient (cost-effective) programs. However, there is, as yet, no information available that would allow such a judgment.

Chapter 7

CONCLUSIONS

This book has presented an evaluation of the therapeutic community known as *414.* On the way to meeting this objective, we have traced the history of the therapeutic community and the development of this modality in the management of addictions. There exists a sizable literature on therapeutic communities that treat people with problems of drug abuse, but little information is systematically available that allows one to make judgments about the efficacy or efficiency of these programs.

Generalizability

Only a small amount of what is currently known about therapeutic communities in the management of addictions was available to us when *414* was initiated in 1970. Nevertheless, the actual structure of *414,* for example, the division of the program into status levels and the use of encounter groups, closely resembles that of other therapeutic communities.

The uniqueness of *414* stems from the fact that the social and drug-using characteristics of the *414* residents are somewhat different from those typically seen in other therapeutic communities. Residents of *414* were white, young, largely from working-class backgrounds, lived in a middle-size city not characterized by urban blight or crowding, and they used intravenously administered amphetamines as their drug of choice. Their careers of drug use averaged about 2 years, which means that they were well-establised users, but still a far cry from the lengthy careers that characterize heroin addicts treated in other therapeutic communities. Nevertheless, some similarities with other therapeutic communities are striking. De Leon et al. (1972) examined rates of arrests among dropouts of Phoenix House. The former residents were of two types: those who entered the program voluntarily and those who entered as a result of coercion (presumably legal) called "nonvolunteers." It would appear that the De Leon et al. volunteers entered treatment on a similar basis to *414* residents. Most notable is the fact that a comparison of rates of arrest for the period before residents entered the Phoenix program and the rates of arrest after the program are largely undifferentiated among categories of residents who spent fewer than 3 months, 3 to 5 months, 6 to 8 months, or 9 to 11 months in treatment. Those who spent more than 12 months in treatment have lower rates of arrest after the program, but there does not appear to be a significant correlation between either rates of arrest or pre—post differences in rates of arrest and time spent in treatment. These findings appear to be comparable to those reported here.

Historically, the therapeutic community has been considered a desirable milieu for people experiencing problems in living. This generality aside, due to the difference in client population between *414* and therapeutic communities for heroin addicts, it is not easy to generalize the results of our evaluation to other programs. Nevertheless, we do wish that other programs would be evaluated along some of the dimensions we have presented here.

We have thought for some time that some of the differences in the characteristics of the residents of our program may account for some of the differences in what actually happened in the *414* community compared to other therapeutic communities (cf. Brook & Whitehead, 1973a). A form of *turnaround* is for persons who have been through the program to stay on as ex-addict staff members (cf. Glaser, 1976). No precise figures are offered in the literature about the number of people who choose to do this, but there is the *sense* that many do.

At *414*, we found relatively little inclination on the part of those who completed the program to stay on as ex-addict staff members. A few did stay for varying periods of time, but, in general, there was little interest in doing so and we feel that the program may have suffered from the relative absence of its potentially most significant role models.

Our recovered amphetamine abusers had real alternatives to staying at *414* and helping others. By the time they reached the reentry stage they were already noticing that other young people of their age were engaged in interesting endeavors. Many decided that they were well enough and sufficiently equipped to go out and get a piece of that action. While their backgrounds are more deprived than those of their non-drug-using peers, they nevertheless do not suffer the extra stigma attached to many heroin addicts such as being black, Puerto Rican, Chicano, or poor (cf. Levy & Green, 1974). In addition, recovered users returned to the larger community at a time of relative economic prosperity and low rates of unemployment. Thus residents of *414* seemed to experience a *pull* to reenter the larger community that was greater than any attraction they felt to *turnaround* and remain as ex-addict staff members.

Past and Future

In early 1973, we decided that *414* ought to be terminated for three reasons: (1) the original objective of seeing whether such a community for adolescent amphetamine abusers could be established had been met; (2) we had enough information and experience on which to base an evaluation; and (3) the need for the service it provided had decreased. Few persons were seeking treatment because the drug crisis of 2 years earlier had diminished.

In most North American communities that still have therapeutic communities for the treatment of drug abusers, the crisis has not passed. There remains a need to provide modalities that can be used to manage persons experiencing the consequences of drug addiction. In their review of available information, Iverson and Wenger (1978) conclude that therapeutic communities "appear to be inefficient . . . and of questionable effectiveness." Some suggestions for the future are offered, but their optimism is restrained. Similarly, Deitch and Zweben (1976) make some reasonable suggestions in terms of which therapeutic communities might be modified in order to facilitate psychosocial maturity among adolescents. Whether such modifications are sufficient to produce a verdict that therapeutic communities are effective and efficient remains an empirical question.

Evaluation and Public Policy

On the basis of our experience, we find it difficult to produce categorical statements about the appropriateness of the therapeutic community or what the future of these communities ought to be. Such questions are not of equal importance to all therapeutic communities. They are only crucial to those communities that exist as matters of *public policy* (cf. Epp & Schaar, 1977). Therapeutic communities that do not obtain public funding, such as Synanon, can exist whether or not they are effective or efficient.

Most therapeutic communities, however, are not of this type. They continue to exist because they receive direct or indirect funding from various levels of government. Such communities should be evaluated as to their efficacy and efficiency and more economic ways of producing the same effect or a greater effect should be sought. If the major benefit of the therapeutic community is that of a port in a storm as we suggested earlier, then such ports may well be provided at a lower cost than is now the case.

For the reasons noted throughout this book, we would have preferred to have made this evaluation more comprehensive (cf. Coulson, Went, Ouellette, Russell, & Kozlinski, 1976; Smart, 1976). Nevertheless, we do take some satisfaction from our efforts. A partial evaluation is better than no evaluation at all. We were apprehensive at first about whether we could successfully recontact many of our former residents. Our success should encourage other investigators to attempt more of these types of studies, rather than abandoning the idea out of a fear of failure.

Epilogue: If You Knew Then . . . ?

We initiated *414* in 1970 with a strong conviction that a therapeutic community was the best way to assist drug-dependent persons. We believed that our efforts would help many residents. We knew that a majority of the residents would not stay very long, but we hoped it would be different. We expected that some of those who stayed a brief time would benefit from their exposure to the therapeutic community, and we were certain that those who stayed longest would benefit the most. As we have seen, some of our pessimistic expectations were fulfilled while our optimistic expectations were dashed.

Had we known at the time of the drug crisis in 1970 what we know now about the probable effectiveness of the therapeutic community we would still have had some difficulty in deciding whether to recommend establishing *414.* From an administrative point of view we would recommend against it because the efficacy of the program is insufficient. We are compelled to agree with others (Amini, Salasnek, & Burke, 1976; Brecher, 1972; cf. Smart, 1976) that treatment, when defined in curative terms, is not a promising alternative in the management of addictions. A different perspective emerges from the point of view of organizations that are publicly funded. They are committed to experimenting with new forms of treatment in order to deliver service more effectively and more efficiently and such a program would make sense as long as the cost-effectiveness of delivering this service could be directly compared with alternative treatments.

Thus, one could recommend involvement in such a publicly funded experience only if there are theoretically or programmatically relevant questions to be addressed and where it is clear that appropriate research designs will be implemented to answer these questions.

In the final analysis, *414* may not have been any more or less effective than a wide range of formal and informal services that are already available. Friends, parents, teachers, police, hospitals, the Salvation Army, churches, and parks may well be as useful as *414* in helping persons in distress to manage their crises. In their own way these other choices provide support and opportunities for persons to mature, for, as Karen Horney indicated more than three decades ago, life itself still remains a very effective therapist.

NOTES

CHAPTER 1

1. Much information on therapeutic communities is not published in journals or books (see Frankel, Brook, & Whitehead, 1977).
2. Recent events involving legal entanglements, conflict with the larger society, and personal tragedy have gained adverse publicity for Synanon and Chuck Dedreich (*Time,* 1977, 1978a, 1979). Now that Synanon's image has been severely tarnished, its contributions to the self-help therapeutic community movement may be neglected. Unchecked authoritarianism and zealous converts to cults can lead to tragedy as occurred in Jamestown, Guyana (*Time,* 1978b). However, there appears to be little basis for generalizing from those events to indictments of the therapeutic community movement as a whole.
3. For example, De Leon (1978, Figure 4, p. 81).

Chapter 2

1. This section on colloquialisms of the therapeutic community is somewhat different from, but based on, an earlier paper (Brook & Whitehead, 1973b).

Chapter 3

1. Another example of this phenomenon is the attention received by acupuncture as a means of treating opiate addiction; see Whitehead (1978) for a review and analysis of the available information.
2. The MMPI also contains three validity scales designed to validate individual tests and aid in interpreting the clinical scales.
3. Interested researchers and clinicians may obtain summary tables from the Addiction Research Foundation, 33 Russell Street, Toronto, Canada (Brook & Whitehead, 1978).

Chapter 5

1. For an indication of the high rates of self-injury among persons who are incarcerated, see Whitehead, Johnson, & Ferrence (1973).
2. Sells and Simpson (1976) examined similar background variables in clustering patients in the Drug Abuse Reporting Program (DARP) conducted by NIMH.
3. See Cohen, Sutker, and Allain (1976), Aron and Daily (1976), and Sells (1974) for a discussion of the commonly used definitions of success and failure in drug rehabilitation studies.

Chapter 6

1. The data for each resident are available to interested investigators (Brook & Whitehead, 1978).

REFERENCES

Alcoholics Anonymous. *Alcoholics Anonymous.* New York: Alcoholics Anonymous World Services, Inc., 1939.

Alcoholics Anonymous. *The twelve steps and the twelve traditions.* New York: Alcoholics Anonymous World Services, Inc., 1952.

Alcoholics Anonymous. Alcoholics Anonymous comes of age. New York: Alcoholics Anonymous World Services, Inc., 1973.

Amini, F., Salasnek, S., & Burke, E. Adolescent drug abuse: Etiological and treatment considerations. *Adolescence,* 1976, *11*(42),281–300.

Anderson, S. B., & Ball, S. *The profession and practice of program evaluation.* San Francisco: Jossey-Bass, 1978.

Aron, W., & Daily D. Graduates and splittees from therapeutic community drug treatment programs: A comparison. *The International Journal of the Addictions,* 1976, *11*(1), 1–18.

Baise, D. V. Adolescent heroin abusers in a therapeutic community: Use of the MAACL to assess emotional traits and splitting from treatment. *Journal of Psychedelic Drugs,* 1971, *4*(2),145–147.

Ball, J. C. On the treatment of drug dependence. *American Journal of Psychiatry,* 1972, *128*(7),873.

Ball, J. C. Sample selection in American follow-up studies of drug abusers. In *Drug dependence: Treatment and treatment evaluation.* Stockholm: Almquist & Wiksell International, 1975.

Barr, H. L. The problem of evaluating the effectiveness of therapeutic communities. *The Addiction Therapist,* 1977, 2(No. 1),38–40.

Bassin, A. Reality therapy at Daytop Village. *Journal of Drug Issues,* 1974, *4*(4),404–413.

Berner, D. M. *X-Kalay: Program description.* Manitoba: The X-Kalay Foundation, mimeo., 1974.

Boorstein, S. A. Psychoanalytic overview of the offender: Implications for therapy. *Psychoanalytic Forum,* 1967, *2*(3),246–256.

Brecher, E. M., & the editors of *Consumer Reports. Licit and illicit drugs.* Toronto: Little, Brown, 1972.

Brewster, J. T., & Garrigues, C. The Mendocino game, rules, policies, modes and techniques. *Drug Forum,* 1974, *4*(1), 15–29.

Brill, L. Comments on the paper Social control in therapeutic communities by Dan Waldorf. *The International Journal of the Addictions,* 1971, *6* (1), 45–50.

Brook, R. C. Research difficulties in clinical settings. (Substudy No. 676) Toronto: Addiction Research Foundation, 1975.

Brook, R. C., & Whitehead, P. C. Colloquialisms of the therapeutic community: Treatment of the adolescent drug abuser. *Federal Probation,* 1973, *7*(4), 46–50. (b)

Brook, R. C., Kaplun, J., & Whitehead, P. C., Personality characteristics of adolescent amphetamine users as measured by MMPI. *British Journal of Addictions.* 1974, *69*, 61–66.

Brook, R. C., Szandorowska, B., & Whitehead, P. C Psychosocial dysfunctions as precursors to drug abuse among adolescents. *Addictive Diseases: An International Journal,* 1976, *2*(3), 465–478.

Brook, R. C. & Whitehead, P. C. 414: A therapeutic community for the treatment of adolescent amphetamine abusers. *Corrective and Social Psychiatry and Journal of Applied Behavior Therapy,* 1973, *19*(3), 10–19. (a)

Brook, R. C., & Whitehead, P. C. Appendices to *Drug Free Therapeutic Community: An Evaluation.* (Substudy No. 982) Toronto: Addiction Research Foundation, 1978.

Burke, L. E. A study of the role of the nurse within the social system of a therapeutic community of a psychiatric hospital. Unpublished Ms.N. thesis, University of Western Ontario, London, 1968.

Campbell, D. T., & Stanley, J. C. *Experimental and quasi-experimental designs for research.* Chicago: Rand-McNally,1963.

Carlin, A. S., Detzer, E., & Strauss, F. F. Psychopathology and nonmedical drug use: A comparison of patient and nonpatient drug users. *The International Journal of the Addictions,* 1978, *13*(3), 337–348.

Casriel, D. *So fair a house.* Englewood Cliffs, N. J.: Prentice-Hall, 1963.

Casriel, D. *A scream away from happiness.* New York: Grosset & Dunlap, 1972.

Casriel, D., & Amen G., *Daytop: Three addicts and their cure.* New York: Hill & Wang, 1971.

Chambers, C. D., & Inciardi, J. A. Three years after the split, In Seney, V. Shorty, & H. Alkane (Eds.), *Developments in the field of drug abuse.* Cambridge, Mass.: Schenkman Publishing Co., 1974.

Charuvastra, V., & Charbeneaux, Z., Drug free therapeutic community: A follow-up study. *Drug Forum,* 1977, *6*(1), 77–83.

Cherkas, M. S. Synanon Foundation: A radical approach to the problem of addiction. *American Journal of Psychiatry,* 1965, *121*, 1065–1068.

Clark, D. H. The therapeutic community: Concept, practice and future. *British Journal of Psychiatry,* 1965, *111*, 947–954.

Cohen, G. H., Sutkerland, P. B., & Allain, A. N. Prediction of successful response to multimodality treatment among heroin addicts. *The International Journal of the Addictions,* 1976, *11*(5), 861–879.

Cohen, S. Methadone maintenance: A decade later. *Journal of Drug Issues,* 1974, *4*(4), 327–331.

Colburn, D. & Colburn, K. Integrity House: The addict as a total institution. *Society,* 1973, *10*(4), 39–45.

Collier, W. V. A profile study on the residents of Daytop Village. *Journal of Drug Issues,* 1973, *3*(1), 10–21. (a)

Collier, W. V. An assessment of prior methadone use by residents of a drug-free therapeutic community. *Journal of Drug Issues,* 1973, *3*(4), 322–332. (b)

Collier, W. V., & Hijazi, Y. A. *Daytop's therapeutic community: A mirrored view.* New York: Daytop Village, Inc., 1973.

Collier, W. V., & Hijazi, Y. A. A follow-up study of former residents of a therapeutic community. *The International Journal of the Addictions,* 1974, *9*(6), 805–826.

Collier, W. V., Hijazi Y. A., Dance, C. R., Broudy, M., Winckler, M., & Forget, A. M. *Daytop Village's drug abuse programs: The 1972 annual report.* New York: Daytop Village, Inc., 1973.

Cooperstock, R. Sex differences in the use of mood-modifying drugs: An explanatory model. *Journal of Health and Social Behavior,* 1971, *12*, 238–244.

Coulson, G., Went, H., Ouellette, M., Russell, S., & Kozlinski, E. Considerations for improving the effectiveness of the therapeutic community approach in the rehabilitation of drug abusers. *Drug Forum,* 1976, *5*(2), 95–113.

Crider, D. M., Willits, F. K., & Bealer, R. C. Tracking respondents in longitudinal surveys. *Public Opinion Quarterly,* 1971, *35*(4), 613–620.

Cruskey, W. R., & Krasner, W. The needle and the boot: Heroin maintenance. *Society,* 1973, *10*(4), 45–52.

Dahlstrom, W., Welsh, G. S., & Dahlstrom, L. E. *An MMPI handbook.* Vol.

2. *Research applications.* Minneapolis: University of Minnesota Press, 1975.

Deissler, K. *Synanon: Its concepts and methods. Drug dependence.* National Clearing House for Mental Health Information, Washington, D.C., *5*, 1970.

Deitch, D. & Zweben, J. The impact of social change on treating adolescents in therapeutic communities. *Journal of Psychedelic Drugs,* 1976, *8*(33).

De Leon, G. Phoenix House therapeutic community: The influence of time in program on change in resident drug addicts. *Proceedings of the 81st annual convention of the American Psychological Association,* 1973, 397–398.

De Leon, G. (Ed.) *Phoenix House: Studies in a therapeutic community, 1968–1973.* New York: MSS Information Corp., 1974. (a)

De Leon, G. Phoenix House: Psychophathological signs among male and female drug-free residents. *Addictive Diseases: An International Journal,* 1974, *1*(2), 135–151. (b)

De Leon, G. & Andrews, M. Therapeutic community dropouts, 5 years later: Preliminary findings on self-reported status. *Addiction Therapist,* 1978, *2*(3 and 4), 74–83.

De Leon, G. & Breschner, G. M., (Eds.) *The therapeutic community: Proceedings of Therapeutic Communities of America planning conference.* Rockville, Md.: Alcohol, Drug Abuse, and Mental Health Administration, 1976.

De Leon G., Rosenthal, M., & Brodney, K., Therapeutic community for drug addicts: Long term measurement of emotional changes. *Psychological Reports,* 1971, *29*, 595–600.

De Leon, G., Holland, S., & Rosenthal, M. S. Phoenix House: Criminal activity of drop-outs. *Journal of American Medical Association,* 1972, *6*(222), 686–689.

De Leon, G., Skodol, A., & Rosenthal, M. S. Phoenix House: Changes in psychopathological signs of resident drug addicts. *Archives of General Psychiatry,* 1973, *28*, 131–135.

Densen-Gerber, J. The Odyssey House method: A comprehensive program for the prevention and treatment of drug addiction. New York: Odyssey House Information Centre, mimeo., 1971.

Densen-Gerber, J. *Odyssey House, Inc. annual report: 1974—our seventh year.* New York: mimeo., 1974.

Devlin, C. J. Daytop Village: A longitudinal review—1963–1974. *The Addiction Therapist,* 1975, *1*(2), 34–39.

Devlin, C. J. Daytop Village: A longitudinal review—1963–1974. *Proceedings of the 31st International Congress on Alcoholism and Drug Dependence.* Bangkok, Thailand: 1975.

Devlin, J. J., & Vamos, P. *An interim report on the characteristics of the portage program for drug dependencies, Inc.* Montreal: mimeo., 1974.

Dupont, R. You alone can do it, but you cannot do it alone. In P. Vamos & J. Brown, *Proceedings of the Second World Conference on Therapeutic Communities.* Montreal: Portage Press, 1977.

Duvall, H. J., Locke, B. Z., & Brill, L. Follow-up study of narcotic drug addicts five years after hospitalization. *Public Health Reports,* 1963, *78,* 185–193.

Eckland, B. Retrieving mobile cases. *Public Opinion Quarterly,* 1968, *32,* 51–64.

Ellinwood, E. H. Amphetamine psychosis I: Description of individuals and process. *Journal of Nervous and Mental Diseases,* 1967, *144*(4), 273–283.

Ellinwood, E. H. Amphetamine psychosis: A multi-dimensional process. *Seminars in Psychiatry,* 1969, *1*, 208–226.

Endore, G. *Synanon.* Garden City, N. Y.: Doubleday, 1968.

Enright, J. B. Synanon: A challenge to middle-class views of mental health. In D. Adelson & B. Kalis (Eds.), *Community psychology and mental health.* Scranton, Pa.: Chandler, 1970.

Enright, J. B. On the playing fields of Synanon. In L. Blank, G. Gottsegen, & M. Gottsegen (Eds.), *Confrontation: Encounters in self and interpersonal awareness.* New York: Macmillan, 1971.

Epp, R., & Schaar, V. A perspective on evaluation of therapeutic communities for drug abuse treatment. *The Addictive Therapist,* 1977 *2*(2), 53–61.

Fairweather, G. W., Sanders, D. H., Maynard, H., & Cressler, D. L. *Community life for the mentally ill.* Chicago: Aldine, 1969.

Frankel, B. G., Brook, R. C., & Whitehead, P. C. *Therapeutic communities in the management of addictions: A critically annotated bibliography.* The Addiction research foundation bibliographic series. Toronto: Addiction Research Foundation, 1977.

Freedman, A., Kaplan, H., & Sadock, B. *Modern synopsia of comprehensive textbook of psychiatry.* Baltimore: Williams and Wilkins, 1972.

Freudenberger, H. J. The staff burn-out syndrome in alternative institutions. *The Addiction Therapist,* 1976, *1*(4), 35–47.

Fryholm, B., Gunne L., & Huitfeldt, B. Prediction of outcome in drug dependence. *Addiction Behaviors,* 1976, *1*(2), 103–110.

Ginzburg, H. M. National institute on drug abuse conducts major opium use study. *Evaluation,* 1976, *3*(1 and 2), 37–40.

Glaser, F. B. Gaudenzia, Incorporated: Historical and theoretical background of a self-help addiction treatment program. *The International Journal of the Addictions,* 1971, *6*(4), 615–626.

Glaser, F. B. Some historical aspects of the drug-free therapeutic community. *American Journal of Drug and Alcohol Abuse,* 1974, *1*(1), 37–52. (a)

Glaser, F. B. Splitting: Attrition from a drug-free therapeutic community. *American Journal of Drug and Alcohol Abuse,* 1974 *1*(3), 329–348. (b)

Glaser, F. B. Special considerations in the utilization of ex-addicts. *The Addiction Therapist,* 1976, *1*(4), 27–34.

Glaser, F. B. The first therapeutic community. *The Addiction Therapist,* 1977, *2*(2), 8–15.

Glasscote, R. M., Sussex, J. N., Jaffe, J. H., Ball, J., & Brill, L. *The treatment of drug abuse: Programs, problems, prospects. Washington, D.C.:* The Joint Information Service of the American Psychiatric Association and the National Association for Mental Health, 1972.

Gold, S. R., & Coghlan, A. J. Effect of residential treatment on adolescent drug abuse: A preliminary report. Paper presented at the meeting of the American Psychological Association, Montreal, August, 1973.

Hill, T. *The Journal.* Addiction Research Foundation, Toronto, 1976, *5*(11), 5.

Holzinger, R. Synanon through the eys of a visiting psychologist. *Quarterly Journal of Studies on Alcohol,* 1965, *26*(2), 304–309.

Hubbard, B., Judd, L., & Avery, R. Psychopharmacologic management of nonopiate mixed substance abusers in an outpatient setting. *The International Journal of the Addictions,* 1978, *13*(3), 383–393.

Iverson, D. C., & Wenger, S. S. Therapeutic communities: Treatment practices in view of drug dependency theory. *Drug Forum,* 1978, *7*(1), 81–103.

Jones, M. The treatment of personality disorders in a therapeutic community. *Psychiatry,* 1957, *20*, 211–220.

Jones, M. *Social psychiatry in practice.* Harmondsworth, England: Penguin Books, 1968. (a)

Jones, M. *Beyond the therapeutic community.* New Haven, Conn.: Yale University press, 1968. (b)

Jones, M. *Maturation of the therapeutic community: An organic approach to health and mental health.* New York: Human Sciences Press, 1976.

Jones, R. E. The characteristics of addicts opting for a self-care program. *Drug Forum,* 1972, *2*(1), 31–42.

Kalant, O. *The amphetamines: Toxicity and addiction. Brookside Monograph of the Addiction Research Foundation,* 1973, No. 5.

Karasu, T., Plutchik, R., Conte, H., Siegel, B., & Hertzman, M. The therapeutic community in theory and practice. *Hospital and Community Psychiatry,* 1977, *28*(6).

Kaufman, E., & De Leon, G. The therapeutic community: A treatment approach for drug abusers. In A. Schecter (Ed.), *Treatment aspects of drug dependence.* Florida: CRC Press, 1978.

Knox, W. Attitudes of psychology students toward drug abuse. *American Psychologist,* 1974, *29*(1), 63–64.

Klinge, V., Vaziri, H., & Lennox, K. Comparison of psychiatric inpatient male and female adolescent drug abusers. *The International Journal of the Addictions,* 1976, *11*(2), 309–323.

Kramer, R. A. *Behavioural characteristics of drug dependency in the young adolescent.* Paper presented to the 30th International Congress on Alcoholism and Drug Dependence, 1972.

Lachar, D. *The MMPI: Clinical assessment and automated interpretation.* Los Angeles: Western Psychological Services, 1974.

Le Dain, G. (Chm.) *Treatment: A report of the commission of inquiry into the non-medical use of drugs.* Ottawa: Information Canada, 1972.

Le Dain, G. (Chm.) *Final report of the commission of inquiry into the non-medical use of drugs.* Ottawa: Queen's Printer, 1973.

Lennard, H. L., & Allen, S. D. The treatment of drug addiction: Towards new models. *The International Journal of the Addictions,* 1973, *8*(3), 521–535.

Lesser, M. E. Perceptions of illness at a therapeutic community for drug addicts: "Legitimate deviancy" or escape? *Social Science and Medicine,* 1974, *8,* 575–583.

Levinson, T. Practical experiences in treatment evaluation through follow-up studies. *Alcoholism: Clinical and Experimental Research,* 1977, *1*(4) 319–323.

Levy, M. H., & Green, H. I. *The family vs drink and drugs.* New York: Institute for the Study of Drug Misuse, 1974.

MacLennan, A. Incest: "A causative factor." *The Journal,* 1975, *4*(5), 1, 4.

Mahon, T. Therapy or brainwashing. *Drugs and Society,* 1973, *2*(5), 7–10.

Main, T. F. The hospital as a therapeutic institution. *Bulletin of the Menninger Clinic,* 1946, *10,* 66–70.

Malcolm, A. I. *The case against the drugged mind.* Toronto: Clarke Irwin, 1973.(a)

Malcolm, A. I. *The tyranny of the group.* Toronto: Clarke Irwin, 1973.(b)

Malcolm, A. I. 1975 The future of the chemophilic society. Paper presented at the Tenth Annual Conference of the Canadian Foundation on Alcohol and Drug Dependencies, Quebec, September 1975.

Marks, P. A., Seeman, W., & Haller, D. L. *The actuarial use of the MMPI with adolescents and adults.* Baltimore: Williams & Wilkins, 1974.

Marshall, J. Quebec addiction body taking on Bon Accord. *The Globe and Mail,* 1978, (21 March), 3.

Maslach, C. Burned-out. *Human Behavior,* 1976, 5(9), 16–22.

McFarlain, R., Cohen, G., Yoder, J., & Guidry, L. Psychological tests and demographic variables associated with retention of narcotic addicts in treatment. *The International Journal of the Addictions,* 1977, *12* (2–3), 399–410.

McKee, M. R., Lehigh, J., & Miller, R. Prognosis for heroin addicts in three rehabilitative programs. *Journal of Drug Education,* 1971, *1*(4), 359–372.

Mowrer, H. O. Therapeutic groups and communities in retrospect and prospect. In P. Vamos & J. Devlin (Eds.), *Proceedings of the first world conference on therapeutic communities.* Montreal: Portage Press, 1976.

Mueller, E. E. Rebels with a cause: A report on Synanon. *American Journal of Psychotherapy,* 1964, *18,* 272–284.

Murphy, J. P., & Densen-Gerber, J. Therapeutic community treatment of addiction. Paper presented at the Scientific Program of the American Psychiatric Association's Annual Meeting, Washington, D.C., May 3–7, 1971.

Nash, G., Waldorf, D., Foster, K., & Kyllingstad, A., The Phoenix House Program: the results of a 2 year follow-up. Unpublished mimeo., 1974.

National Institute on Drug Abuse (NIDA). Conducting follow-up research on drug treatment programs. *National Institute on Drug Abuse Treatment Program Monograph No. 2.,* 1977.

O'Brien, W. B. The family milieu as the epicenter of drug abuse treatment. In E. Tongue, A. Magistretti, & A. Vincze (Eds.), Papers presented at the International Conference on Drug Dependence, Rome, May 1976.

Odyssey House Information Centre. Odyssey House program for pregnant addicts and addict females. New York: 12 pages, mimeo.(a)

Odyssey House Information Centre. The Odyssey House adolescent program. New York: 4 pages, mimeo.(b)

Odyssey House Information Centre. A new direction: The Odyssey House parents program. New York: 3 pages, mimeo.(c)

Ogborne, A. C., & Melotte, C. An evaluation of a therapeutic community for former drug users. *British Journal of Addiction,* 1977, *72,* 75–82.

Patalano, F. Psychodiagnostic testing in a therapeutic community for drug abusers. *Psychological Reports,* 1976, *3*(9), 1279–1285.

Pin, E, Martin, J., & Walsly, J. A follow-up study of 300 ex-clients of a drug-free narcotic treatment program in New York City. *American Journal of Drug and Alcohol Abuse,* 1976, *3*(3), 397–407.

Popour, W. Lessons in living: R. A. P. *Corrections Quarterly,* 1972, Michigan Department of Corrections, Lansing.

Portis, B., & Powell, J. *Systems analysis of student flow in secondary schools.* London: Research and Publications Division, School of Business Administration, University of Western Ontario, 1972.

Rachman, A. W., & Heller, M. E. Anti-therapeutic factors in therapeutic communities for drug rehabilitation. *Journal of Drug Issues,* 1974, *4*(4), 393–403.

Rapaport, R. N. *Community as doctor.* London: Tavistock Publications, 1960.

Rohrs, C. C., Goldsmith, B., & Densen-Gerber, J. Odyssey House: Drug free treatment failures. New York: Odyssey House Information Centre. 16 pages mimeo., 1971.

Rohrs, C. C., Murphy, J. P., & Densen-Gerber, J. The therapeutic community: The Odyssey House concept. In J. D. Zarafonetis (Ed.), *Proceedings of the international conference on drug abuse.* Philadelphia: Lea and Felinger, 1972.

Rosenthal, M. S. Phoenix House: A therapeutic community for the treatment of drug abusers and drug addicts. In L. Brill & E. Harms (Eds.), *The yearbook of drug abuse.* New York: Behavioral Publications, 1973.

Rosenthal, M. S., & Baise, D. V. Phoenix houses: Therapeutic communities for drug addicts. *Hospital and Community Psychiatry,* 1969, *20,* 43–46.

Sack, M. Therapeutic community movement. *Journal of Psychedelic Drugs,* 1974, *6*(2), 169–171.

Sack, M. (Chm.) *North American Association of Therapeutic Communities: 1975 directory of therapeutic communities in North America.* Seattle: The Stonewall Press, 1975.

Salasnek, S., & Amini, F. The heroin addict in a therapeutic community for adolescents: A cultural "rip-off." *Journal of Psychedelic Drugs,* 1971, *4* (2), 138–144

Schriven, N. The methodology of evaluation. In *Perspectives of curriculum evaluation. American Educational Research Association Monograph Series on Curriculum Evaluation.* Chicago: Rand McNally, 1967.

Sells, S. B. *Studies of the effectiveness of treatments for drug abuse.* Vol. 3. Cambridge, Mass: Ballinger Co., 1974.

Sells, S. B. Reflections on the epidemiology of heroin and narcotic addiction from the perspective of treatment data. In J. D. Rittenhouse (Ed.), *The epidemiology of heroin and other narcotics.* Rockville, Md.: National Institute on Drug Abuse Monograph 16, 1977.

Sells, S. B., & Simpson, D. (Eds.) *The effectiveness of drug abuse treatment: Further studies of drug users, treatment typologies, and assessment of outcome during treatment in DARP.* Vol. 3. Cambridge: Ballinger Co., 1976.

Sells, S. B., Simpson, D., Joe, G., Demaree, R., Savage, L., & Lloyd, M. A national follow-up study to evaluate the effectiveness of drug abuse treatment: A report on cohort 1 of the DARP five years later. *The American Journal of Drug and Alcohol Abuse,* 1976, *3*(4), 545–556.

Shelley, J., & Bassin, A. Daytop Lodge: A new treatment approach for drug addicts. *Corrective Psychiatry,* 1965, *11*(4), 186–195.

Smart, R. G. *Outcome studies of therapeutic communities and halfway house treatment for addicts. The International Journal of the Addictions,* 1976, *11*(1), 143–159.

Smart, R. G., & Jones, D. Illicit LSD users: Their personality characteristics and psychopathology. *Journal of Abnormal Psychology,* 1970, *75*(3), 286–292.

Smart, R. G., & Whitehead, P. C. The uses of an epidemiology of drug use: The Canadian scene. *The International Journal of the Addictions,* 1974, *9*(3), 373–388.

Stang, H. J. Three year follow-up of 100 vagrant adolescent drug abusers in Oslo. *Acta Psychiatrica Scandanavia,* 1977, *55,* 381–390.

Stephens, R., & Cottrell, E. A follow-up study of 200 narcotic addicts committed for treatment under the Narcotic Addiction Rehabilitation Act (NARA). *The British Journal of Addiction,* 1972, *67*(1), 45–54.

Stricker, G. Implication of research for psychotherapeutic treatment of women. *American Psychologist,* 1977, *32*(1), 14–22.

Svalastoga, K. Longitudinal research designs. *International Journal of Comparative Sociology,* 1970, *11*(4), 283–291.

System Sciences, Inc. *Descriptive report and analysis of Daytop Village, Inc.* Bethesda, Md.: System Sciences, Inc. 1973.(a)

System Sciences, Inc. *Descriptive report and analysis of Phoenix House, Inc.* Bethesda, Md.: System Sciences, Inc. 1973.(b)

System Sciences, Inc. *Descriptive report and analysis of Odyssey House, Incorporated.* Bethesda, Md.: System Sciences, Inc. 1973.(c)

Time magazine. Life at Synanon is swinging. *Time,* December 26, 1977, p. 18.

Time magazine. The snake in the mailbox: Challenging Synanon can be hazardous to health and wealth. *Time,* October 23, 1978a, p. 25.

Time magazine. Nightmare in Jonestown. *Time,* December 4, 1978b, pp. 10–15.

Time magazine. Cult wars on Capitol Hill. *Time,* February 19, 1979, pp. 46–47.

Tripartite Conference. Regulation and the law: A general discussion. *Alcoholism and Alcohol Education,* 7(5), 7–10.

Vaillant, G. A twelve-year follow-up of New York narcotic addicts I: The relation of treatment to outcome. *American Journal of Psychiatry,* 1966, *122,* 727–737.

Vaillant, G. Outcome research in narcotic addiction—Problems and perspectives. *American Journal of Drug and Alcohol Abuse,* 1974, *1*(1), 25–36.

Volkman, R., & Cressey, D. R. Differential association and the rehabilitation of drug addicts. *American Journal of Sociology,* 1963, *69*(2), 129–142.

Waldorf, D. Social control in therapeutic communities for the treatment of drug addicts. *The International Journal of the Addictions,* 1971, *6*(1), 29–44.

Wathey, R., & Densen-Gerber, J. Incest: An analysis of the victim and the aggressor. *The Addiction Therapist,* 1976, *1*(4), 48–58.

Weppner, R. S. Matrix House: Its first year at Lexington, Ky. *HSMHA Health Reports,* 1971, *86*(9), 761–768.

Weppner, R. S. Some characteristics of an ex-addict self-help therapeutic community and its members. *British Journal of Addiction,* 1973, *68*(1), 73–79.

Wexler, H. K., & De Leon, G. The therapeutic community: Multivariate prediction of retention. *American Journal of Drug and Alcohol Abuse,* 1977, *4*(2), 145–151.

Whitehead, P. C. Head or brain?: Drug use and academic performance. In J. E. Gallagher & R. S. Lambert, *Social process and institutions: The Canadian case.* Toronto: Holt, Rinehart and Winston of Canada. 1971.

Whitehead, P. C. Acupuncture in the treatment of addiction: A review and analysis. *The International Journal of the Addictions,* 1978, *12*(6), 1–16.

Whitehead, P. C., & Brook, R. C. Social and drug using backgrounds of drug users seeking help: Some implications for treatment. *The International Journal of the Addictions,* 1973, *8*(1), 75–85.

Whitehead, P. C., Johnson, F. G., & Ferrence, R. G. Measuring the incidence of self-injury: Some methodological and design considerations. *American Journal of Orthopsychiatry,* 1973, *43*(1), 142–148.

Winer, B. *Statistical principles in experimental design.* New York: McGraw-Hill, 1971.

Yablonsky, L. The anticriminal society: Synanon. *Federal Probation,* 1962, *26*(3), 50–56.

Yablonsky, L. *The tunnel back: Synanon.* New York: Macmillan, 1965.

Yablonsky, L. Synanon: A breakthrough in the treatment of drug addiction. *Journal of Drug Issues, 1*(2), 153–159.

Yablonsky, L., & Dederich, C. E. Synanon: An analysis of some dimensions of the social structure of an antiaddiction society. In D. M. Wilner & G. G. Kassabaum (Eds.), *Narcotics.* New York: McGraw-Hill, 1965.

AUTHOR INDEX

SUBJECT INDEX